Field Dressing

Big Game

Field Dressing
Big Game

James Churchill
Illustrations by Doug Pifer

Stackpole Books

Copyright © 1989 by Stackpole Books

Published by
STACKPOLE BOOKS
Cameron and Kelker Streets
P.O. Box 1831
Harrisburg, PA 17105

First Edition, 1989

Printed in the United States of America

10 9 8 7 6 5 4 3 2 1

Photographs by Joseph J. Branney (pronghorn antelope); Irene Vandermolen
(bighorn sheep); Leonard Lee Rue III (mountain goat, timber wolf, wolverine); Len
Rue, Jr. (caribou, javelina); Neal & Mary Jane Mishler (moose); Denise Hendershot
(mountain lion); and Florida Game & Fresh Water Fish Commission (alligator).

Library of Congress Cataloging-in-Publication Data

Churchill, James E., 1934–
    Field dressing big game / James Churchill.
        p.   cm.
      ISBN 0-8117-2282-1
      1. Game and game-birds, Dressing of. 2. Big game animals.
    I. Title.
SK283.8.C48   1989
799.2'6—dc19   88-32369
                                                        CIP

To Michael Paul

The world needs more good leaders.

To Courtney Michelle

The world needs more good leaders.

Preliminaries

Rule number one

The very first thing to do upon bringing down your quarry is to make sure it is dead. This is a humane consideration as well as a matter of your personal well-being. So before you lay down your gun to begin field dressing, determine whether the animal has stopped breathing. Watch for a minute or two. If you're in doubt, shoot the animal again. You want to kill it quickly without ruining its cape, if you plan on taking home a trophy as well as the meat. On a deer, then, shoot through the neck just ahead of the shoulders.

Bears are especially dangerous, even small bears, and I wait an hour before approaching them. Sometimes, though, time is short. Approach the animal from the rear and, with your rifle ready and at hand, poke it with a stick. The eyes of a dead bear are usually open, glazed and lifeless. If the eyes are shut, or open and bright, shoot the animal again. Drive the bullet down between the shoulder blades to break the spine and completely disable the bear, since head and neck shots will ruin it for mounting.

Equipment

Taking gear into the field creates a problem: weight. But the big-game hunter can easily carry a knife, small game saw, 50 feet of stout rope, and a small rope hoist in his pack. This equipment will suffice to carve even the largest animal into manageable portions.

Knives. You can start an argument among any group of experienced hunters by insisting on a particular size or style of knife. Hunting knives can be classified according to whether they have folding or fixed blades, and drop point, clip point, or trailing point blades. Drop points are considered best for skinning and are also very serviceable for other hunting chores. Clip point blades are best for working the skin from small areas, like the base of an antler, but they, too, satisfy general hunting needs. The trailing point blade is most useful for cutting up meat after it has been skinned and quartered; it would be a poor choice as a general-purpose hunting knife.

My favorite is a folding knife with a 4-inch drop point blade. It is light and compact enough not to be a burden, sturdy enough to cut through the sternum of a deer or bear, and delicate enough to fillet out tenderloin and carve meat from the bone.

Whatever knife you choose to take into the field, you'll want to keep it razor-sharp, so carry a small whetstone in a pocket.

Game saw. A game saw isn't an absolute necessity, but when you're handling elk or moose, it will save time and toil, especially for cutting the pelvic arch, severing leg bones, and separating the backbone and ribs. Available from outdoor suppliers, a saw weighs only a few ounces — not much to carry. Some hunters take along a hatchet or small hand axe for cutting firewood and other tasks; either can be used instead of a saw for cutting heavy bone.

Rope. Nylon rope and a small rope hoist are used to roll the animal on its back for field dressing, and to hang quarters or the whole carcass. Quarter-inch nylon rope is strong enough for hunting needs.

My rope hoist can lift up to 600 pounds but itself weighs less than a pound. Still, you don't need to carry one all the time. Leave it in camp and take it to the kill site when you need it.

In the field, you should have a packframe and a hoist along with your knives and other tools.

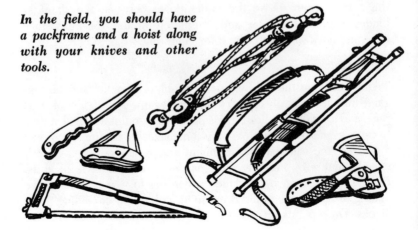

You may want to carry a length of heavy string into the field; it's handy for tying off leaky tubes, among other uses.

Plastic. Ten-gallon plastic bags are large enough to hold the heart, liver, and kidneys of big game, keeping them clean while you do the rest of the field dressing. A folded 6- by 12-foot plastic sheet will keep the skinned-out pieces of meat off the ground when the animal is butchered in the field.

From most western sport shops and outdoor mail-order firms you can get mesh game bags, which allow air to circulate and cool the meat but keep the flies off. These are usually kept in camp, for use when the meat is brought in and hung to cool.

Packframe. Getting meat and trophies from a remote area to the road usually means carrying it out yourself. With a hunter's packframe, H frame, or trapper's packbasket, a 200-pound man can carry about 60 to 80 pounds on his back, at least for a short distance. Steep terrain, deep snow, boggy ground, or thick forest reduces the load that can be carried safely. If you intend to carry an entire quarter at a time, use the packframe.

For trophies. In the field you'll need a tape measure, notepaper and pencil, and camera. Back at camp you should have noniodized salt, fleshing knife, screwdriver, pliers, stout cord for tying up hides,

In camp, your equipment should include a gambrel, a stretcher, and a fleshing tool.

and a roll of paper towels. If you plan to stretch the skin of a wolf or wolverine, borrow a stretcher from a trapper friend or buy one from a trapping supply house.

Handling the meat

One of the most pressing and sometimes perplexing problems with big-game meat is cooling it rapidly enough that it doesn't spoil.

This is often done in four steps: take out the intestines; take off the hide; cut the carcass into the smallest practical pieces; move the meat to the coolest spot available. Depending on the size of the animal and the air temperature, however, you may not have to skin the animal or cut it up. And under some circumstances you can cut the animal into quarters without removing the skin. Study the appropriate chapter for proper handling of each animal; remember, your goal is to cool the meat quickly.

Do not cover meat with plastic bags unless it is thoroughly cooled out, since plastic keeps the heat from escaping. But plastic bags are very useful for keeping meat clean while you transport it to a cool place where it can be taken out of the bags.

Flies are often a problem early in the season. Prepare for this by taking mesh game bags and black pepper into the field with you. Place as much of the skinned carcass as possible in game bags; whatever meat can't be protected in this way can be coated with a thick layer of black pepper. A pound of pepper will cover the exposed meat on an unskinned deer or bear; you'll need 5 to 10 pounds for larger game.

Butchering. If you don't mind the nominal cost, the easiest way to get your meat cut up is to take it to a butcher. But some people say commercially prepared game meat just isn't as good because the butcher doesn't have time to remove all the fat and tallow, which do not freeze well and shorten the freezer life of the meat. Or the butcher may trim off too much meat. But there's still another reason to do your butchering: It is a logical conclusion of the hunt.

The first step in butchering is to age the meat. Deer and other small hoofed game are easily managed because you can hang the entire carcass with its skin intact. Larger game will have been cut into quarters and perhaps even boned out for ease of transport from the field.

Average cooling time for skinned animals at 38°F

	Hours		Hours
Antelope	17½	Javelina	11
Bear	28	Moose	30
Caribou	23	Mountain goat	19
Deer	19	Mountain lion	18
Elk	23	Sheep	20

Cool your meat properly. Refrigerate alligator meat as soon as the animal is skinned.

Hang the meat in a shed, cellar, garage, or cooler and age it at 38°F according to the table. During the aging process, the sugar in the muscles changes to lactic acid. This weakens the tissues, making the meat more tender. It also enhances the flavor.

After the meat has aged, strip the skin off the carcass, hang it up by the hindlegs, saw it down through the center of the backbone, and cut it into the standard butchering cuts shown. Double wrap with a layer of plastic wrap and cover with freezer paper.

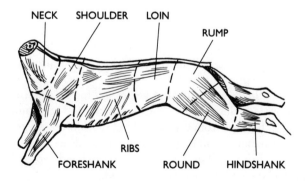

These standard butchering cuts apply to most big-game animals.

Big game animals, especially elk and moose, may be too large for your freezer unless they are boned out. Boned out meat keeps well and takes up only a fraction of the space that standard cuts require. Keep the pieces large by following the natural muscle divisions where possible. The backstraps can be cut from the backbone in two large strips and then reduced to cuts of cooking size. Rib meat and other trimming cuts can be cut into stew pieces or put through a hand grinder for hamburger.

If possible, chill all meat before cutting it into pieces. Chilled meat is firm and will slice evenly.

Be sure to trim out bloody meat and bone chips from the meat. To make bloody meat edible, soak it in cold water for a few hours. Pick out any hairs, which debilitate the flavor of even the best cut. Most wild game is covered with a thin layer of tissue that should also be taken off before the meat is cooked.

Caping antlered game

One of the reasons for hunting is to collect a trophy head for mounting. Select a skilled taxidermist to do the work. But even the best practitioner cannot make a good mount if he doesn't have a good skin to work with. You need to know how to skin out the cape and care for it until it gets to him.

Take your camera and tape measure with you into the field. Immediately after the animal is down, shoot closeups of all sides of the animal's head: front, sides, from below the head, directly down on the top. Then back off and shoot some full-body shots from different angles. These pictures will help the taxidermist reproduce your animal's natural appearance.

All hoofed animals are caped out according to certain principles; the exceptions are described in the directions for each animal. If possible, take the cape from the animal before skinning or gutting it to lessen the chance of spoiling the fur with blood stains, grime, and dirt. Some hunters just skin the cape out to the head and lay it back out of harm's way without severing the head.

Start by selecting an appropriate knife, one with a rather stiff blade about 4 inches long. Have a stone on hand as you skin and use it to keep the knife very sharp.

Cape all animals for a shoulder mount. Even if you later choose to have a neck mount (which is seldom seen now), this caping proce-

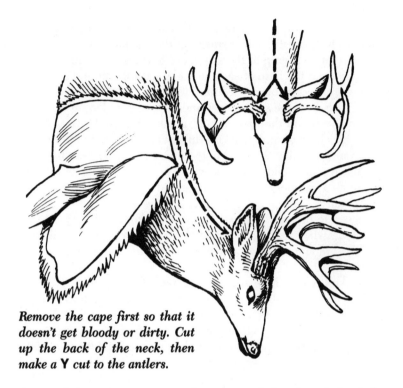

Remove the cape first so that it doesn't get bloody or dirty. Cut up the back of the neck, then make a Y cut to the antlers.

dure will be correct. Start at the center of the chest behind the forelegs. Cut straight up over the animal's back and down the other side to join the cuts. Circle cut the skin of the forelegs about 4 inches down—this skin will be part of the cape.

Next, cut up the back of the neck to the point midway between the ears. Then make a Y cut to the base of each antler.

Starting at the shoulders, peel the skin forward up the back of the neck to the last neck joint. Cut around the neck meat at this point and twist the head to separate the head from the neck. This method leaves the skull in the cape. It can be skinned out later, either by you or by the taxidermist. He will also remove the skull plate with the antlers attached.

Skinning out the head. Sometimes you have to skin out the head to keep it from spoiling, or so that you can transport it out of the wilderness. Proceed slowly. If you haven't already severed the head from the body when taking the cape, do so now.

Skin the head to the base of the ears and cut them off, right next to the skull. Leave the ear cartilage in the ear for now—it will be taken out later. Then pull the skin loose to the antlers and pry the skin away from the base of each antler. A screwdriver and a pair of pliers will expedite this procedure. Lift the skin with the pliers and push the blade of the screwdriver under the skin to loosen it. Work completely around the base of both antlers. You could use a knife with a thick blade, but then be careful not to cut the skin into strips.

Continue skinning the head to the eyes and cut the skin free. Be sure to leave the eyelids. To sense where to make the cuts for freeing the eye area without cutting off the eyelids, push your fingers into the eyeball.

Proceed to the lips and nose, keeping the knife right against the skull bone when cutting tissue so that you don't cut through the skin. The lips and nose are cut loose from the bone and left attached to the skin.

The skull is now bare and you can saw off the antlers. Leave a good bit of the skull for the taxidermist by sawing horizontally through the eye sockets to the back of the head. If you don't have a saw in the field, chop off as much of the nose area as you can without disturbing the skull plate to lighten the head for transport; once in camp, you can neaten up the job with a saw. When the skull plate is removed, clean off the brains and flesh and salt it well. The bone will not spoil, but salt will draw out the moisture, letting it dry faster without as much odor.

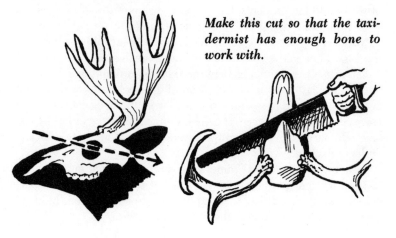

Make this cut so that the taxidermist has enough bone to work with.

Now flesh the cape. Using a fleshing knife, remove any large chunks of meat and flesh. Next, turn the ears inside out and remove the cartilage. One way is to push the ear down over a broom handle or other round stick. Then peel the ear skin down and trim out the cartilage by pushing the knife blade between the cartilage and the skin. Working from the inside, split the lips in several places so that salt can penetrate.

Finally, spread the cape out, hair side down, and pour salt on the skin. Spread it around to all parts of the hide and work it in. A deer, antelope, sheep, or goat cape requires about 5 pounds of salt. An elk's cape takes about 10 pounds; a moose's, about 15 pounds. If you choose not to salt your trophy, freeze the head and cape as soon as possible.

A full mount. If you want the full body mount of a large hoofed animal, the entire skin and cape must be removed as a unit. To make sure the taxidermist can reproduce the trophy as it looked in life, take measurements of the body before it is field dressed. Then dress the animal.

The first skinning cuts extend from the field dressing opening to the hooves. Slit up the back of the front legs and the back of the rear

Take these measurements for a full body mount before gutting.

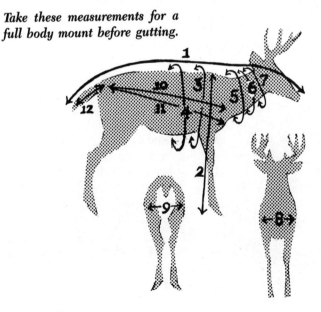

legs from the field dressing cut to the hooves. Free the hooves at the first joint, but don't cut through the skin—the hooves should be attached to the skin. Then work the skin off the legs and peel it to the cape. Slit the cape up the back of the neck, as for removing the cape, but don't cut around the chest. The cape is skinned out from the back of the neck and left attached to the body skin. The head can be skinned out, as described above, or left to the taxidermist. Pull the tailbone out of the skin and open the skin so that it doesn't spoil. A taxidermist's work will be easier if you use the dorsal-cut method for skinning out a full body mount. Slit the skin from the tail up the center of the back to the head. Work the skin downward over the body and legs. Skin out the head as usual; you can make cuts up the back of the legs if necessary.

The hide can now be left to drain for a while if it's bloody or wet. But before it dries, you must flesh it and salt it well. A moose or elk will require about 25 pounds of salt; a caribou, about 15; and a deer, antelope, sheep, or goat, about 10 pounds.

Spread the skin out, hair side down, and pour half the salt into the center. Rub it into the hide with your hands. The extremities, head skin, and the base of each hoof should receive an extra portion of salt. Roll it up and incline one end so that it drains.

Let it cure in the coolest place available. The salt will draw out moisture, which should be allowed to run off so that the skin will dehydrate—a necessary part of the curing procedure. Just make sure the liquid doesn't run off onto your gear. Scrape and resalt the hide in about 72 hours, using the other half of the salt.

Antlers only. Some hunters want just the antlers for a trophy. To remove them from the head in the field, start by skinning off the hide between them, down the front to the eyes, and down the back of the skull. This will be tanned and used to cover the area between the antlers when they are mounted on the plaque.

Then, using a saw or hatchet, cut horizontally from the eye sockets to the back of the skull. Take off plenty of bone with the antlers so that the taxidermist has something to work with when he attaches the horns to the plaque. If you can't get the antlers intact from the field, they can be sawed apart. Saw right down the centerline so that half the bone is still attached to each antler. But remember that after they are cut apart, antlers can't be scored for the Pope and Young or the Boone and Crockett record book.

Small Hoofed Game

Deer

Range. White-tailed deer are found in all the contiguous United States, in all the southern Canadian provinces, and in Mexico. The majority are found from the Mississippi River states eastward. Mule deer and black-tailed deer live in the states west of the Mississippi River, in Alaska, in the western Canadian provinces, and along the west coast of Mexico.

Size. Deer vary greatly in size, from the collie-sized Key deer in Florida to the whitetails and mule deer. A mature northern whitetail buck is 70 to 85 inches long and stands 30 to 44 inches high at the shoulder. The weight of a buck varies from 150 to 300 pounds, with 240 pounds being the average. Exceptionally large whitetails have been known to weigh nearly 500 pounds. A mature whitetail doe weighs 60 to 210 pounds, with 160 pounds being average. The doe is 63 to 79 inches long and about 27 to 33 inches high at the shoulder.

Pelage. The white-tailed deer has two coats. The summer coloration is reddish brown, and the winter color is gray with dark markings on the face and ears. Summer hair is wispy; winter hair is thick, hollow, and sturdy. The underparts, including the underside of the tail, which gives the deer its name, are white in all seasons. The buck has antlers that are shed every year.

The mule deer also has a reddish-brown summer coat and a gray-brown winter coat. It is most easily distinguished from the whitetail by the length of its ears, which are about 11 inches long, compared with 7 inches for the whitetail.

The black-tailed deer is a subspecies of the mule deer and has very similar pelage.

The fawns of all species are reddish brown with white spots.

Behavior. Deer are shy, nervous animals that stay in or near cover at all times. Always alert, they have excellent senses of smell and hearing, and can see well enough to identify a moving enemy at a considerable distance. When alarmed, whitetails can run 30 to 50 miles per hour.

Deer spend most of their time feeding and lying down chewing their cud. Buck deer are solitary, but the doe and her fawns may stay together in family groups. In winter, deer may band together with other family groups in swamps or evergreen thickets called deer yards.

Deer make loud blows or snorts to warn of danger. Fawns bleat, and bucks make grunting sounds when chasing does in estrus.

Habitat. The white-tailed deer prefers thick woods or swamps bordering on a field or other opening where food is abundant. It can survive in agricultural areas or in nearly unbroken forest if necessary. The whitetail is almost always found near a pond, lake, or river.

The mule deer spends its life along the fringes of a mountain meadow in a mixed forest of aspen and evergreen. It typically descends the mountains to feed and water, and goes back upslope to bed down.

The black-tailed deer lives in thick forest; its habitat resembles that of the whitetail.

Food. An adult deer consumes about 6 to 8 pounds of food every day. Deer are primarily browsers and feed on more than 110 kinds of woody plants. Favorites include yew, white cedar, hemlock, mountain ash, red maple, staghorn sumac, dogwood, wintergreen, and wild cranberry. Deer also eat grass, favoring alfalfa and clover grass. Because of the shortage of food in winter, deer may be forced to eat evergreen needles. They often lose 30 percent of their body weight over the winter.

Reproduction. The doe breeds in her second year, except on good range, where she may come in heat her first year. The buck is sexually mature in his second year but may not breed because the dominant buck in his territory will chase him away from the receptive does.

Deer breed in late October or November. The gestation period is about 196 days. Fawns—usually twins, sometimes triplets—are born in late May or June. Deer can live twenty years or more, but in most areas a ten-year-old deer is considered old because of hunting pressure and winter kill.

Deer

The hunter of white-tailed and mule deer takes part in a venerable tradition. Like the prehistoric hunter, he can come home with deerskin for clothing, venison for the table, and a trophy for his home.

Gutting. After the deer is down, roll it onto its back and prop it in place with tree branches or rocks. Starting at the hollow of the rib cage, make a knife slit just through the skin from the ribs to the crotch. If it's a buck, free the penis and scrotum from the belly. Lay them out of the way, but don't cut them off. Then go back to the forward end of the cut and carefully make a short cut through the belly muscles. Stick two fingers through the cut inside the belly, lift the muscles from the intestines, and with the knife held sharp edge up, cut the muscles and meat along the length of the belly to the crotch to open the chest and abdomen.

Cut down to the pelvic bone at the crotch. If you can't split the pelvis, cut around the anus and female organs from the outside and pull the tubes inside. Carefully cut the colon and urethra away from the upper body and lay their ends outside the body cavity. Then roll the paunch and intestines out of the body cavity. Cut through the diaphragm as you remove the abdominal contents.

Make this first cut carefully so that you don't puncture the intestines. Use your fingers to guide the knife.

Pull the guts well away from the carcass.

Next, remove the heart and lungs: Reach into the chest cavity, cut the windpipe and esophagus as far forward as possible, grasp the severed ends of the tubes, and pull the heart and lungs out of the chest cavity, cutting tissue as necessary.

Roll the deer over and leave it belly down for at least 10 minutes to let the blood drain from the body cavity. If fresh, clean water is available, rinse the body cavity out to remove all blood and impurities. But no great harm will come to the meat if you cannot clean out the body cavity: The film of blood will harden to a crust and keep the meat from drying out or spoiling. If the deer was gut shot, however, and the body cavity is contaminated by visceral matter, be sure to clean it with grass, leaves, or whatever is available.

Separate the heart from the lungs and the liver from the intestines and clean them up: Remove the tissue surrounding the heart and trim the gall bag from the liver. Then put them in a plastic bag. When you get home, slice the heart open to remove the blood from the valves. The liver also can be sliced to remove blood clots. Both heart and liver should then be immersed in cold water.

Speed gutting. You have shot a buck. Night is falling, and if you don't reach the road in 15 minutes, you will spend the night in the woods. This procedure will get you out in time.

Lift up the deer's external sex organ and cut it off. This creates a hole in the belly. Reach in, lift the tissue to keep the knife point out of the intestines, and make a slit up the belly to the ribs. Reach into the forward end of the slit and cut the diaphragm loose. Pull hard on the severed diaphragm to start the paunch and intestines coming out of the cut—hard enough to tear the guts loose from their attachments inside the abdomen. Use the knife to cut tissue you can't tear. Rip the guts out and cut the colon just forward of the pelvis to free the intestines. This can be done in less than 5 minutes. Now drag the deer out. The heart and lungs are still in the chest; remove them in camp. Then split the pelvis and remove the anus. Wash and wipe out the body cavity as soon as possible.

Cooling the meat. In the field, cool the meat by propping the body cavity open with a short stick wedged between the ribs. Hang it in the shade where air can circulate around it. Keep flies off by using game bags or coating the meat with black pepper.

At camp, you can cool deer by elevating the body on three or four small logs, packing the body cavity with ice, and then covering the whole works with a canvas. In 24 hours the ice will have melted and the deer will be thoroughly cooled. It will then keep for several days if the temperature is 45°F or less.

Skinning and caping. Deer should not be skinned until you are where the carcass can be processed: The hide will keep the meat clean. If you haul the deer on the outside of a vehicle, cover it with a plastic bag or other protective coating.

There are two skinning methods. You can hang the deer by the hindlegs and, starting the skin at the hind

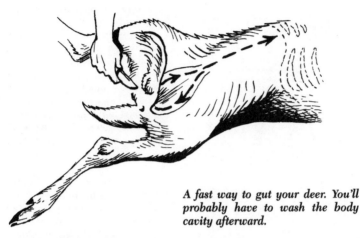

A fast way to gut your deer. You'll probably have to wash the body cavity afterward.

hocks, pull it down over the body (see *Elk*). But it is just as easy to skin, cape, and butcher a deer hanging by its head, which is the way deer are hung (because it lets the body cavity drain). Here's the procedure.

Hang the deer so that the head is slightly above your eye level. Be sure the animal is held securely by a heavy rope or chain wrapped around its horns or, if a doe, around the neck just below the head.

Cut off all four legs. The front legs are severed at the knee, and the hindlegs at the hock. Make skinning cuts up the inside of each leg from the severed joint to the field dressing cut. Now go to the back of the deer's neck and make a cut from 4 inches below the head to the center of the shoulders. Then turn the knife 90 degrees and join this cut to the field dressing cut on the deer's chest. Pull upward on the shoulder skin to free the cape from the body. Tie it to the antlers to keep it out of the way. Skin the rest of the deer by pulling downward on the skin,

cutting tissue if necessary. A pair of pliers will help get the hide started, and you can then peel the entire hide off without resorting to the knife. Set the skin aside.

Now return to the cape. Sever the head from the body at the first vertebra and salt the cape with at least 2 pounds of noniodized salt, or take it immediately to the taxidermist. A third alternative is to freeze it as soon as possible.

Once the cape is taken care of, spread the hide out flat, hair side down, and salt it well. Use about 10 pounds of salt for a large deer. Pour the salt in the center of the hide, spread it out to the edges, and rub it in well. Then roll the hide up and let it "work" for at least 72 hours; resalt it and let it drain for a week before you send it off to the tanner.

Butchering. Deer can be butchered very easily at home. Although the deer is hanging head-up — not the conventional way for butchering — it works out well enough: The animal can be quartered a piece at a

time and the quarters placed on a table for butchering.

Remove the front legs by cutting the tissue between the leg and the body. A deer doesn't have a shoulder joint, so the leg can be removed with a knife very quickly. Pull outward as you cut. Next, cut across the backbone just behind the ribs to remove both hindquarters and the loin in a single piece. Now cut the rest of the carcass free by severing the neck just in front of the shoulder.

Use any clean, expendable wooden surface for a butchering table. Make sure it's at least 3 feet square. A piece of ½-inch-thick plywood or an old wooden table will work just fine.

The legs will yield steaks, roasts, stew meat, and even hamburger. Cut each front leg into three pieces: the upper shoulder, the lower shoulder, and the shank. Remove both hindlegs by cutting across the carcass just ahead of the legs, then sawing down through the backbone to separate them. Saw off any bone extending below the meat on the hindlegs.

Make the next cut across the carcass at the last forward rib. Stand this center portion of the carcass up on end and saw it down through the center of the backbone. (If you have a small deer, you can omit this step.) Saw away the breast section, which can be used for roasts, stew cubes, or hamburger. Then cut the loin and ribs into chops: Cut across the backbone between the disks for the loin chops and between the ribs for the rib chops. Finish butchering the carcass by severing the neck from the head. Wash off any hair with cold water and wipe the meat dry before cooking it or grinding it up.

Hang the deer by the head, and then make the skinning cuts.

Pronghorn antelope

Range. The pronghorn antelope is found in Alberta, Saskatchewan, Montana, Wyoming, North and South Dakota, Nebraska, Colorado, Texas, New Mexico, Arizona, Nevada, California, Oregon, Washington, and Idaho. Populations are very high in Wyoming.

Size. A mature buck antelope is 4 to 5 feet long and about 3 feet high at the shoulder, and weighs 100 to 120 pounds. A doe antelope is 3½ to 4½ feet long and weighs 80 to 100 pounds.

Pelage. The antelope is reddish tan over the upper body and the outsides of the legs. The belly, the insides of the legs, and the rump patch are white. The throat is white with two dark tan bands. The buck's face is dark brown to black, with a black neck band on the upper neck and lower jaw. The female is lighter colored in these areas. Newborn fawns are gray.

The buck has black horns that are 10 to 15 inches long, but the female's horns usually measure less than 4 inches.

Behavior. Pronghorn antelope live in herds on the open plains. They are always alert and their eyes scan the territory constantly, looking for enemies. They sleep for only short stretches. Antelope have a good sense of smell and usable hearing, but they depend upon their exceptional eyesight to protect them. They can spot moving objects miles away.

Antelope can run faster than any other animal in North America. A playful gallop is 25 miles per hour; a usual running speed is 50 miles per hour. Some individuals can reach 60 to 70 miles per hour. They also walk rapidly and can swim well if they have to. Although they are most active in early morning and late afternoon, antelope often feed at night.

Herds usually number four to a dozen or more animals, which might be does, fawns, and a mature buck or two. Some older large bucks stay by themselves, and some herds are made up of bucks only.

Antelope can withstand extremes in temperature because of their hollow hair, which is controlled by unique muscles in the tissue holding the hair. An antelope can lower the hair tightly against its body for almost perfect insulation in cold weather; when it's warm, the animal can raise the hair to let air circulate against the skin.

Antelope fawns bleat; when disturbed, does and bucks snort.

Habitat. Pronghorn antelope prefer wide-open, treeless territory of rolling plains, grasslands, and sagebrush flats, and most are found at elevations between 5,000 and 6,000 feet above sea level. Good antelope habitat includes a source of water, since they drink nearly every day.

Food. The antelope eats sagebrush as a dietary staple; in winter, it may be nearly the only food available. Rabbit brush, bitter brush, and juniper are also important browse plants. Common antelope foods include native grasses and such weeds as thistle, dandelion, and sour dock. The antelope has the four-part stomach common to grazing animals and lies down to chew its cud after an hour or so of feeding.

Reproduction. Doe antelope breed in their second year. The rut takes place from August to October. Buck antelope become near-lunatics when the rut approaches, sometimes standing listlessly by themselves, sometimes galloping wildly over the plains for no apparent reason. They round up a harem of four to a dozen does and defend them against other bucks. Although there is much threatening and posturing, fights are uncommon.

The does are usually bred in September, but the gestation period is eight months long, so the young are not born until the following May or June. Single births are most common, although twins and triplets are not unusual. The young weigh about 8 pounds when born and develop rapidly. In two weeks they can follow their mothers and run up to 20 miles per hour. The fawns stay with the does until the following spring — or even longer if the doe doesn't breed again.

Antelope live about seven or eight years.

Pronghorn antelope

The pronghorn antelope is relatively small and can be handled by one person. It is dressed, skinned, and cut up much like other grass eaters (such as deer), with one distinction: It has an extremely fragile hide that will deteriorate if it's not properly handled.

In warm weather, antelope spoil quickly, so they must be field dressed and cut up as soon as possible. Fortunately, they are usually hunted on the plains, accessible to vehicles.

Before you hunt the antelope, check with the state game laws. Some states require that animals be kept intact, except for field dressing, until they are registered.

Field dressing. Field dress the antelope as you would a deer. Roll the antelope on its back and open the belly cavity from the rib cage to the crotch. Use just the tip of the knife to cut through the belly skin and muscles. If your animal is a buck, excise the male organ from its attachment.

Then cut down to the pelvic bone between the legs and, using a sturdy knife, split the pelvis. Circle cut around the anus (and the vagina if the animal is female) to free the tubes from the skin. Remove the rectal and bladder tubes from their seat over the pelvic arch. Pull the tubes forward far enough to lay them down outside the body cavity.

Next, split open the rib cage by cutting through the sternum to the throat. Reach in the rib cage and cut off the windpipe. Pull on it to take out the heart and lungs. Pull out the intestines. (You will have to cut the

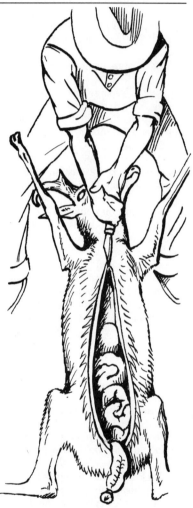

After you've slit the animal from ribs to crotch and tied off the rectal tube, split the sternum to open the rib cage. You'll then be able to remove the internal organs.

21

diaphragm to get to these organs.) Put the heart and liver in a plastic bag to keep them clean for now, but cut them open and wash them as soon as possible. Roll the antelope on its belly to let the body cavity drain.

Back at camp, hang the animal up by the hindlegs. You can hang it by attaching a separate rope to each hindleg, or slit the gambrel joints, push a pipe through the slit, and then attach the pipe to your rope.

Taking the cape. Cape the buck and skin out the head at the same time. First, make the customary cuts around the body behind the shoulders, slit up the back of the neck to the head, and then make a Y cut to each horn. Work the skin from the shoulders down the neck to the head. You can cut off the head and take the cape and head to the taxidermist. But you may decide to skin out the head yourself. You can do this quite easily with the antelope hanging in the head-down position. Follow the directions given for caping out antlered game. Scrape the cape and salt it, using about 1 pound of salt. Since the hide will quickly spoil, get the cape to the taxidermist as soon as possible.

Skinning. After the cape and head have been taken care of, slit the antelope down the inside of each hindleg to the field dressing cut. Work the skin down the legs to the back and cut off the tail at its base. By just pulling on the skin, you should be able to peel it to the shoulders. Then cut off the front legs at the knee joint and slit the skin up the inside of the leg to the field dressing cut. Go back to the body skin and pull it downward to strip it completely off the animal.

An easy way to cape out your antelope buck. Hang the animal by the hindlegs before you make the caping cuts. Make the first cut around the antelope's body.

Scrape the skin to remove any flesh and fat, and then salt it well, using at least 5 pounds of salt, unless you can freeze it immediately. Get the skin to the taxidermist or tannery as soon as you can, before the hide deteriorates. The skin makes poor leather but an appealing wall hanging.

Butchering. With a meat saw, saw the animal down the center of the backbone to divide it into halves. Then divide the antelope into standard butchering cuts. Trim all bloodshot meat and fat and wrap the antelope meat for freezing.

Wild sheep

Range. Rocky Mountain bighorn sheep live in the mountains of all states west of the Dakotas, and in Alberta and British Columbia. Dall's sheep are found in northern British Columbia, the northwestern Yukon, and Alaska mountain ranges. Stone's sheep live in northern British Columbia and the southern Yukon. Desert bighorns are found in the Baja Peninsula and parts of Mexico.

Size. The Rocky Mountain bighorn ram is about 5 to 6 feet long and about 3 to 3½ feet high at the shoulder. Bighorns weigh 150 to 300 pounds. Dall's sheep and Stone's sheep weigh 180 to 225 pounds, but stand about as high as the smaller bighorns.

Pelage. The bighorn has a gray-brown coat with a white to yellowish rump patch. The muzzle, the area around the eyes, and the backs of the legs are pale to white. The Dall's sheep is pure white, but the Stone's sheep is darkish to nearly black, except for the belly, rump, and the backs of the legs. The lambs of the bighorns are gray with a dark stripe on the back. The lambs of Dall's and Stone's sheep closely resemble the adults.

Mature rams of all three species have large curled horns. Female wild sheep have smaller horns.

Behavior. Wild sheep spend most of their time looking down on the world from some high mountain perch, usually above the timberline at elevations 8,000 or more feet above sea level. They have excellent eyesight, good hearing, and a fair sense of smell. Wild sheep can run across mountainsides with incredible agility, jumping from ledge to ledge at high speeds. They can also swim well if necessary.

Sheep move most in the daytime, spending the dark of night sleeping. They stay in herds or bands that are segregated by sex and age: ewes and lambs in one, rams in the other. Only during the breeding season do the rams join the ewes. When a ewe is about to give birth, she goes off by herself and remains alone until the lamb is old enough to join the band.

Lambs bleat, and mature sheep occasionally blat.

Habitat. Sheep prefer gently angled mountainsides and grassy basins. Nearby will be a higher area of rock rubble and steeply angled cliffs for an escape route in case they encounter predators or hunters. Sheep live very sedentary lives in their home territory unless heavy snows cover their food and force them into lower elevations. In desert regions they are sometimes forced into lower elevations by the lack of water.

Food. The wild sheep is a grazer, living almost entirely on grass if it's available. Vetch, needle grass, wheat grass, and fescue are primary foods. Clover and a variety of forbs are also taken. When the snow is deep, the sheep eats sagebrush, greasewood willow, and alders. If forced to, it will nip off twigs of juniper, spruce, and fir. Tree buds also are an important food in the early spring.

The desert sheep eats whatever grass and shrubs are available, and even eats cactus.

Reproduction. The female wild sheep breeds when she is two years old, but the ram does not breed until he is three. For most wild sheep, the brief rutting season is in late November and early December, but desert sheep start breeding as early as August. The mature rams fight fierce battles for territory during the rutting season. They don't fight for the favors of the ewes, since both ewes and rams are entirely promiscuous.

The gestation period is six months long, and most lambs are born in May and June. Single births are the rule, although twins are occasionally born. The new lamb weighs about 8 pounds at birth and is 11 inches high. If the lamb is female, she stays with her mother for years, but a male will leave the mother after two years.

Wild sheep can live about twelve years, but few survive that long in their rugged environment.

Wild sheep

A great many sheep are taken on mountainsides so steep that one false move might push the sheep over the edge. It's necessary to make a platform for the body of the sheep so that it doesn't slip away down the hill. The platform can be made of rocks, deadwood, or even a hollow in the snow.

Caping out. Most sheep are taken for the head, so the cape is removed first. Take a sharp knife and cut behind the front legs clear around the body. Circle cut around the front legs at the shoulder. Then slit the cape up the back of the shoulders and neck to a point about 3 inches behind the horns. Starting at the shoulders, pull the hide of the cape

forward to the head. If the animal is still warm, the hide will pull very easily. Then, keeping the hide forward so that it doesn't get contaminated, cut the head from the body at the last joint of the neck—cutting down to the bone all around the neck, then twisting the head until it breaks loose. Most hunters pack the cape and head back to camp and skin out the head there.

At the back of the head, cut from the back of the neck to the base of each horn. Use a screwdriver or knife blade to pry the skin loose around the base of the horn and down the forehead. When you get to the eyes, cut very close to the skull to keep the eyelids and eyebrows on

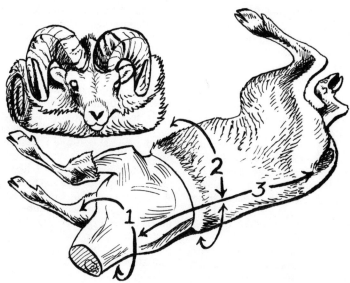

Remove and roll up the cape first, then make quartering cuts.

The sheep will be easier to transport if you bone it out in the field. To bone out a hindquarter, hang it by the hoof from a rock, and cut off the meat in large chunks.

the skin. Push your fingers in the eyeballs so that you can feel where to make the cuts around the eyes. Cut the nose cartilage on the inside to make sure the nose outer skin is not nicked. Leave the lips on the skin. Keep the knife right against the skull bone when you are removing the hide to avoid skinning cuts.

Butchering. Once the cape has been taken, you can dress the animal using the conventional method for field dressing hoofed game. The carcass is usually cut into quarters without first being skinned. In exceptionally rough terrain, you might bone the carcass before trying to move it.

Skinning. If game laws specify that all the meat be retained, even the meat between the ribs, the animal must be completely skinned so that you can remove the meat from

the bones. The sooner you skin after the kill, the easier it will be. Skin the animal on its side, starting at the field dressing cut. Cut each hindleg off at the hock and slit up the inside. (The front legs were already skinned when the cape was removed.) Peel back the skin and cut the meat off the bone. Use plastic bags to protect the meat as it is removed. Then roll the animal over and repeat the procedure.

Skinning the quarters. I like to cut the sheep into quarters with the skin on. Then, still on the mountain, I skin the quarters and cut the meat off the bone a quarter at a time. A 250-pound sheep will have about 80 pounds of boned meat to carry out. Most any hunting knife will do the job of boning out meat, but a sharp, flexible 4-inch blade is an excellent choice.

To cut the caped but unskinned animal into quarters, first sever the neck ahead of the shoulders. Then feel for the last rib and cut between it and the adjoining rib from the field dressing cut to the backbone. Do this on both sides and then sever the backbone to divide the animal into halves. Pull the wool back from the knife cuts so that you don't push it into the meat.

Stand the halves on end. Use a saw or hatchet to cut down the center of the backbone (or use a heavy hunting knife to sever the ribs on either side of the vertebrae) to divide the animal into quarters.

Bone the quarters, starting with a forequarter. Hang it by a hoof—if you can't find a tree, you may have to hang the animal from a rock—and pull off the strip of skin left after removing the cape. Starting at the lower leg, slice against the bone to remove the shank meat up to the shoulder. Follow the division between the muscles to keep the meat chunks as large as you can. Each forequarter yields three pieces: upper shoulder, lower shoulder, shank.

The hindquarters are much larger, but they can be boned out the same way. Hang each one by a hoof

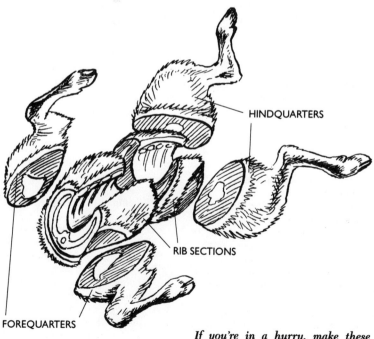

HINDQUARTERS

RIB SECTIONS

FOREQUARTERS

If you're in a hurry, make these quick cuts in the field. Save the skinning and butchering for camp.

and cut the meat from the bone in large chunks. The hindquarters can be divided into three pieces each: rump, round roast shank, hind shank. Fillet the neck meat from the bone. Keep the knife sharp. Following along the bone, slice away the loin meat on either side of the backbone and the meat on the ribs. Be sure to remove the meat between the ribs, as it is choice roasting meat for a victory celebration.

Quick cuts. Some hunters hack the sheep into pieces without skinning or boning it, preferring to skin it after they have the meat safely in camp. This is the fastest way to get the carcass ready to carry and is worth considering. First, cape and field dress the sheep. Then, without skinning, cut the carcass in half by slicing between the last two ribs and severing the backbone. Cut off the neck just ahead of the shoulders.

Sever the front and rear legs from their attachments at the shoulder and hip joints. If the rib sections are still too large to handle, divide them in half by cutting between the ribs. Reduce the rear section to two quarters by splitting the backbone, and if needed, divide the hindlegs by separating the thigh from the hip at the shank joint.

Mountain goat

Range. The mountain goat is found in high rugged mountains in Alaska, the Yukon, the Northwest Territories, British Columbia, western Alberta, Washington, Idaho, and Montana. Northwestern Wyoming, Utah, and western Colorado have small populations. The Black Hills area of South Dakota has a herd of about 400 animals at the state's highest point, Harney Peak. Washington has the highest population in the lower forty-eight states.

Size. The mountain goat billy is 5 to 6 feet long and about 2¾ to 3½ feet high at the shoulder. Billies weigh 125 to 300 pounds, but trophies have been collected that weighed 500 pounds. The females — nannies — are only somewhat smaller.

Pelage. The mountain goat has a shaggy white coat that sometimes darkens to near yellow. The coat is made up of 6-inch-long guard hairs over a 4-inch-thick layer of wool. The goat has long chin whiskers and spiky black horns. Its eyes, hooves, and nose are also black. The hump on the mountain goat's back is present in both sexes, but it is more noticeable on older males. The sexes are hard to distinguish otherwise, since both have horns and whiskers and are about the same size.

Behavior. The mountain goat usually lives on steep mountainsides, but it sometimes descends to mineral licks at lower elevations. Its senses of smell, hearing, and sight are very keen. The mountain goat is a calm animal and, it is thought, completely silent. If necessary, it runs at a slow controlled gait that allows it to traverse mountainsides without losing its footing. It can swim well.

Goats are active during daylight hours. The billy goat may stay by himself, but the nannies and kids are often found in small bands. The billies join the bands during the breeding season.

Habitat. One scientist has observed that the mountain goat is the only animal that still lives in the Ice Age. Superbly equipped to withstand cold and negotiate precarious footing, it prefers to live high on the peaks where the ice and snow never melt. It spends most of its time on barren rock slopes, but moves into high-altitude short-grass meadows to feed. Its bed may be a small platform on a rock promontory with a 500-foot drop on either side.

Even though icy winds howl across its domain summer and winter, the goat does not suffer because of its heavy coat, which cold cannot penetrate. Only rain bothers the goat, forcing it to seek shelter in a cave or under an overhang.

Food. Mosses and lichens are the mountain goat's common year-round foods; willows, conifers, and aspen are staple winter foods. Grasses, forbs, and the leaves of such shrubs as bearberry make up the summer ration. If necessary, the goat will descend to the tree-line to find food, where — goatlike — it makes do with whatever vegetation is available.

Reproduction. The female breeds at two and a half years of age. The rut takes place during November and December. The males bully each other during the rut, but most times the posturing doesn't develop into a fight. If a fight does occur, one billy is often injured by the sharp, spiky horns of the other.

After a six-month gestation period, the young are born in May or June; usually a single kid is born, although twins are not infrequent. The kid weighs about 6 pounds when born. It can walk in twenty minutes and can follow its mother within two hours. The kids start eating grass within a week and are weaned by July or August. They stay with their mothers in a band for a year or more.

A mountain goat can live for ten or twelve years in the wild.

Mountain goat

The beautiful white coat of the mountain goat makes a prized wall hanging or rug. As soon as the animal is down, position it so that it will not get bloody while it is being caped and dressed. The goat can be handled like the bighorn sheep, but the following method will keep the skin and cape almost bloodless.

Skinning. Lay the animal on its back and skin out a strip about 1 inch wide from the crotch up the center of the belly as far as the front legs. Avoid cutting into the body cavity—you want only to skin the animal at this time.

Working from this strip, remove the complete skin as in skinning a full body mount. Slit up the inside of the front legs and the rear of the hindlegs from the field dressing cut to the hooves. Make the cuts adjacent to the long legging hair so that they won't show. Sever the hooves without cutting the skin at the ankle joint, or if you don't want the hooves, circle cut around the legs just above the hooves.

Work the skin from the body, spreading it out from the carcass as you work. Take off the cape by cutting the skin between the shoulders up the back of the neck. Lay the skinned carcass on stones or a plastic sheet to keep it clean.

Wash the skin and cape in clean water if it has picked up some blood or dirt. The sooner you do this, the easier it will be to remove the stains. Starting at the tail end, roll up the skin and tie it or place it in a plastic bag. Now it's ready to pack out. If you have to make more than one trip to get everything back to camp, take your trophy on the first run. As soon as possible, unroll and salt the skin so that it doesn't spoil.

Gutting. Mountain goats are gutted like deer. Starting at either the chest or the crotch, slit the belly muscles from one end to the other. Cut down to the pelvic bone between the hindlegs and split the pelvic bone to expose the rectal and urethral tubes. Excise the tubes by cutting around the anus, and pull

If you first skin out a strip of hide from the belly, you'll find it easier to skin out the rest of the goat.

them forward. If you have a billy, remove the male organ with the tubes. Start pulling the intestines out of the body cavity, cutting tissue where necessary. You'll have to cut the diaphragm loose to remove the intestines. Run the knife all around the body cavity where the diaphragm is attached to the body wall.

After you remove the intestines, take out the contents of the chest cavity. The heart is edible; place it in a plastic bag to keep it clean until you can slice it open and wash it with cool water.

Quartering. Because you'll likely have to carry the goat to camp on a packframe, you will want to lighten your load. If time does not permit boning, at least quarter the animal.

First, pull the legs away from the body and cut between the body and legs to expose the joints. Sever the legs from the body at the joints. With all four legs removed, cut the carcass in half behind the ribs.

Place each piece of the carcass in a plastic bag before tying it to the packframe.

Skinning out the head. If you have time and a sharp knife, skin out the head and saw the horns from the skull before you send the head to the taxidermist. Use great care in skinning the head, but do it in the customary manner: Slit the skin up the back of the head to the ears and cut them off at the base. Continue pulling the skin forward to the horns and cut around them at the base to free the skin. Work the skin forward off the face, being careful around the eyes and lips. When the head skin is free, scrape off the excess flesh and slit the lips from the inside so that the salt will penetrate. The head will keep for a week or more.

Saw the horns from the skull by making a horizontal cut from the eyes to the back of the head. Clean the brains and flesh from the skull and horns for quicker curing.

The long legging hair will help hide the skinning cuts when the animal is mounted.

Large Hoofed Game

Elk

Range. The Rocky Mountain elk, the most numerous of the subspecies of American elk, is found from southern British Columbia and Alberta south to central Arizona and New Mexico, and from South Dakota west to central Washington. Rocky Mountain elk have also been transplanted to a dozen states and provinces outside their natural range. Roosevelt elk are found along the Pacific coast in Washington, Oregon, northern California, and Vancouver Island, British Columbia.

Size. An adult bull elk measures 7½ to 9 feet long and 56 to 68 inches high at the shoulder, and may weigh 650 to 1,000 pounds. The cow is 7 to 7½ feet long and 48 to 56 inches high at the shoulder; she usually weighs 500 to 650 pounds.

Pelage. The bull elk has a dark brown neck and head. The sides of its body are pale brown or yellowish gray, with a large white or yellowish patch on the rump. The cow's coloration resembles the bull's but tends to be darker. Calves are brown with yellow or white spots.

The bull elk has large antlers that sometimes reach 5 feet in length, with a 5-foot spread. He sheds his antlers each year.

Behavior. Elk are wary animals that live in herds. They are sociable and tolerate one another very well—except when the bulls are in rutting season or when the pregnant cows are about to calf. Most herds are composed of cows and calves and a bull or two. Some bulls form herds, some are solitary.

The elk walks about 6 miles per hour but can run 45 miles per hour (the usual running gait is a pacing trot that covers ground amazingly fast). It is a good swimmer. It has excellent senses of hearing and smell, and its eyesight is keen, although it cannot identify nonmoving objects very well.

Most active at dawn or dusk, the elk tends to be more nocturnal than diurnal. Its usual activity is feeding; it spends most of its time either eating or traveling to find food. When the elk isn't hungry or thirsty, it finds a shady location to doze and chew its cud.

Bull elk bugle during the rut, and cows bark, squeal, and chirp. Calves bleat when very young.

Habitat. A very adaptable animal, the elk can thrive in wet forests as well as in desertlike areas. Generally it summers in high country, where cool breezes abound and insects are few. About the first of July, when the open areas of the high country dry up, the elk takes to the timber. It remains in high-country timber until the November snows fall, when it descends to midelevations, usually made up of conifer forests. When the snows are heavy, it moves down to the valleys. Even then it forages as high on the slopes as it can.

Food. The elk is both a grazer and a browser, and it seems to digest weeds, grass, and woody plants with equal ease. But it prefers grass and forbs, which constitute 85 percent of its diet in the spring, summer, and fall. A large bull elk eats 20 pounds of food each day.

Reproduction. Cow elk can breed in the second year of life, although many do not conceive during the first year of sexual maturity. Cows three to seven years old produce the most calves. Yearling bulls can breed, but probably do not get a chance until they are large and strong enough to drive a herd bull away from the harem.

Mating occurs in late September and October. The gestation period is 247 to 262 days long, so the calves are born around June 1. Most births are a single calf; twins are born about once in every 100 births.

Elk can live for twenty years or more but rarely attain that age because of the stresses of winter and predation.

Elk

Elk have the annoying habit of dropping in places that will never appear on the list of Best Butchering Billets. They often drop on the side of a mountain, miles from the road, or worse yet, in a valley between two mountains, with the road on the other side of the higher mountain.

Caping out. You should take the cape before the animal is dressed to keep it from getting bloody. But if you're inexperienced or slow, gut first.

Leave the neck and shoulder skin for the taxidermist. Make the first cut around the elk's body just be-hind the front legs. Starting from that cut, slit the back of the neck to the ears. Notice that no cuts are made on the lower neck when a head is mounted. Include 8 inches of skin on the upper front legs.

Next, make a Y cut from the ears to the base of each antler. Now skin out the upper shoulder and neck by rolling the hide forward to the base of the head. Try to clean-skin the hide, leaving the meat on the neck instead of on the hide. Cut the head off where it is attached to the neck.

If you can get the head to a taxi-dermist or freeze it right away, you

Elk are caped in the standard manner. Pull the hide to the last neck joint and sever it, leaving the skull in the hide.

can leave the cape and head intact. If not, you must skin out the cape from the head before your trophy spoils. Taxidermists advise against this procedure because it requires painstaking work, but most hunters can do it if they don't rush.

Start by cutting the ear bases from the head on the underside of the skin. Then work the skin off the antler bases. The hide usually must be pried from the antler area with a screwdriver or similar tool.

Next, work the skin forward to the eyes. Use great care not to cut the eyelids or make any extra holes in the hide when you cut the eyelids loose from the eye sockets. Trim the nose cartilage well back inside the nose and leave the flesh of the lips intact, cutting along the bone of the jaws.

The cape is now free. Remove the ear cartilage, trimming it out with a knife, or pulling it out with your fingers or a pair of pliers after you have partially separated it from the ear skin with a screwdriver or knife blade. Turn the ears inside out and salt the cape thoroughly or freeze it if you can't deliver it to a taxidermist within a day or two.

The antlers have to be sawed off the skull. Make a horizontal cut from the eye sockets backward to the rear of the skull. This leaves enough bone so that the taxidermist can mount the antlers without much trouble.

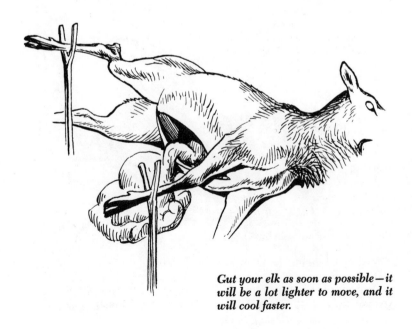

Gut your elk as soon as possible—it will be a lot lighter to move, and it will cool faster.

Gutting. A cow elk is a huge animal, and a bull elk is even bigger. Gutting one when you are alone can be a gigantic task, but you can do it. If you can roll the elk on its back, you'll find the work easier. Some hunters carry a small rope hoist and 50 feet of ¼-inch nylon rope. If the animal falls near a tree, they can usually turn it over with a rope hoist.

On its side. An elk can be gutted lying on its side. First cape out the head. Then use forked sticks or ropes to hold the upper legs straight out from the body. If necessary, cut the legs off at the knee and hock. Start the field dressing cut at the solar plexus. Make the first cut just through the skin from chest to crotch. Free the penis and scrotum from the belly, then lay them back out of the way without cutting them off. Continue the first cut to the anus. Then go around the anus, sticking the knife deep enough to sever the tissue that supports the rectal and urinary tubes. If the animal is a cow, cut around the vagina and anus both unless the law requires that evidence of sex be left on the animal.

Then go back to the chest. Slit through the belly muscle far enough that you can get two fingers inside to hold the intestines away. Slit the belly open, then roll out the paunch and intestines. You will have to cut the diaphragm to free the abdominal contents. After the intestines and liver are out on the ground, pull them out of the way. Elk liver is usually not eaten.

Next, reach inside the chest, cut off the windpipe, esophagus, and tissue holding the heart and lungs, and remove them. Cut the heart free

from the lungs and put it in a plastic bag.

Quartering. Usually quartering is done in the field before the animal is skinned because the hide will keep the quarters clean on their way to camp. Cut off the front legs at the knee and the rear legs at the hock.

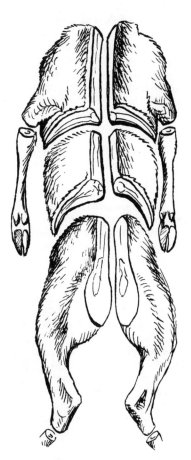

Cut up the elk with the skin on to keep the meat clean.

Big game

Starting at the back rib, count forward three ribs, and then cut between ribs three and four from belly to backbone. Do this on both sides, then chop through the backbone to sever the carcass in two. Next, cut the head from the neck at the base of the skull, if it hasn't been caped out. Cut the neck off the carcass at the shoulders.

Stand the halves on end and cut down through the center of the backbone: Lay an axe blade at the center of the spine and pound on the back of the blade with a heavy stone. Bag the quarters for transportation. Each quarter of a 400-pound elk will weigh about 80 pounds—a load many hunters can carry for short distances.

Boning out. If you are backpacking, it's expedient to fillet the meat and leave the bones and trimmings behind. This is easier after the elk has been quartered. Use a sharp knife to cut the meat away from the bone. Remove the meat on the legs by following the separations between the muscles, keeping the pieces as large as possible.

Bone out the loin by cutting on each side of the backbone down to the ribs. Then turn the knife blade at a 90-degree angle and cut the loin loose from the bone. Remove the meat over the ribs by slicing along the outside of the ribs. Trim out the meat between the ribs, too.

Working alone. Elk can be boned out without being either gutted or quartered. When you must handle a large animal alone, this is often the best way to proceed.

First, skin out the cape as outlined in the section on caping antlered game. Remove the head at the base of the skull and set it out of the way.

Next, cut off the front legs at the knee and the rear legs at the hock. Skin out a section of each leg just above the cut so that the hide can later be easily pulled down and off. To hold the legs away from the animal's midsection, elevate them with ropes fastened to a tree, or use forked sticks.

Then make a skinning cut from the anus to the cape. Also cut down the inside of each leg. Peel the hide from the upper half of the elk and lay it back out of the way. Now remove the front leg: Push it upward and cut the attachments at the shoulder joint. Bone out the shoulder to make it easier to carry.

Next, remove the hindleg: make a cut at the crotch down to the pelvic bone. Then slice along the pelvis to the hip joint. Sever the leg at the hip joint by cutting the tissue holding it in place. Bone out the hindleg right away to help it cool.

Now fillet the loin and rib meat. Slice as close to the backbone as possible, cutting straight down to the ribs. Then turn the knife at right angles to cut the loin away from the bone. It will come off in a long strip from the hips to the neck. This is very choice meat.

Shave the rib meat away from the ribs, starting from the backbone. You can take off this entire sheet of meat in one large slab; just turn it back as you shave it away from the bone. Trim the meat on the neck away from the neckbones. When the meat has been removed down to the belly, cut it off, roll it up, and put it in a clean bag.

Now turn the animal over and skin

and bone out the opposite side.

To remove the heart and tenderloins from the animal, you must gut it, but now it is much lighter and easier to handle.

With a hoist. If you have a hoist available, you can skin and butcher elk just like cattle. First gut the elk on the ground, then make a slit on the hindlegs at the gambrel joint, between the leg bone and the tendon just above the hock. Insert a metal pipe or hardwood pole through these slits and fasten it to a rope or chain. Use a sturdy, high-slung hoist capable of lifting the elk clear off the ground.

Skin the animal as you raise him. First make a circle cut around the hindlegs just below the cross pipe.

(Be careful not to cut the tendon that supports the carcass.) Slit up the inside of the hindlegs to the crotch. Start peeling the skin away from the hindlegs by lifting a flap of skin and shaving away the tissue that holds the skin to the meat. Skin both hindlegs, lifting the carcass so that it is always at a convenient height.

Cut the tailbone off at the base and leave the skin on it. Work the hide downward to the shoulder and then remove the cape if you want to keep it. If the cape won't be kept, peel the hide downward to the base of the head and cut the head off.

Then saw the carcass in half down the center of the backbone and butcher it in the conventional manner.

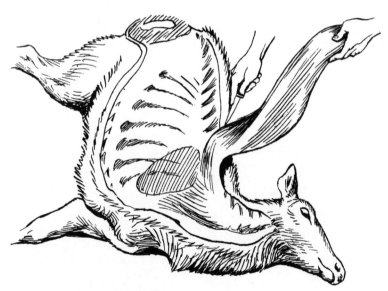

Strip the meat from the elk's carcass one side at a time.

Caribou

Range. All American caribou are of the same species, although they have some dissimilarities related to location. Barren-ground caribou are found across the far north from Alaska through the Yukon and the Northwest Territories, sometimes in herds numbering 100,000 or more. Mountain caribou are found in the Cassiar Mountains of northern British Columbia, with some as far south as Washington and Idaho. Quebec caribou are found in northern Quebec and the surrounding provinces, and woodland caribou are found in the timbered regions of central Canada and the Maritime Provinces.

Size. The caribou bull is 6 to 7½ feet long and stands 46 to 51 inches high at the shoulder. It weighs 300 to 400 pounds. The cow is 5¼ to 6¾ feet long and 42 to 46 inches high at the shoulder. The cow weighs 195 to 260 pounds. Woodland caribou are usually the largest.

Pelage. Males and females are similar in color—dark gray to brownish gray. Their winter coats tend to be lighter than summer fur. The forehead, neck, abdomen, patch behind the shoulder, and edging around the feet are white. The calves are reddish brown.

Both the bull and the cow have huge antlers, but the female's are smaller than the male's. Caribou antlers have flattened prongs and forks or beams; the bow prongs are unusually large and often flattened. Barren-ground caribou have slightly larger antlers than woodland caribou. Antlers more than 4 feet in length with a 4-foot spread have been taken from all four subspecies. The largest caribou antlers in the record books were taken from a woodland caribou killed in Labrador; they measured 5 feet long with a 5-foot spread.

Behavior. The caribou is almost completely diurnal except during the dark period of winter, when there is little or no daylight in the

Arctic. Caribou are herd animals, and are almost constantly on the move. Barren-ground herds migrate hundreds of miles from their summer calving grounds to their winter feeding grounds. Woodland caribou are also restless but don't move nearly as far.

The animal travels rapidly across the terrain at an easy trot. When frightened, it can run fast enough to escape wolves, about 30 miles per hour. It seldom walks or gallops. The caribou is a strong swimmer and will not hesitate to swim broad, raging rivers.

The caribou has strong senses of smell, eyesight, and hearing but apparently lacks the intelligence to interpret what its senses tell it. It will often stand and stare at a hunter until it is bagged.

Although the caribou is usually a docile animal, a bull will fight fiercely in the rutting season, and a cow will attack wolves in defense of her young.

Caribou of either sex may utter a grunt now and then but are usually silent.

Habitat. Barren-ground caribou live on the far northern tundra, and woodland caribou live in conifer forests. The mountain caribou prefers the northern regions or wooded mountainous terrain. Barren-ground caribou summer in the Arctic tundra and winter in the evergreen forests to the south. Woodland caribou spend most of the year in forests but seem to prefer swamps, bogs, and muskegs in the forests rather than the upland regions.

Food. Summer food for the caribou is mostly caribou moss, grass, and leaves of willow, birch, and blueberry. In winter it eats lichens and moss, which it finds by pawing through the snow. Sometimes it moves to timbered areas to browse evergreen needles and aspen twigs.

Reproduction. The female caribou breeds in her second year. The bull also is capable of breeding in the second year and services ten to fifteen cows. The rutting season is late September or early December. After a thirty-one-week gestation period, the young are born in late May or June. Caribou usually have only one calf; occasionally twins are born.

Caribou live about four to five years in the wild but have a potential longevity of thirteen years.

Caribou

Caribou live in places so remote that just getting them to a boat or airplane for the ride to camp is a day's work. They may be skinned in the field or cut unskinned into quarters. Consider leaving the head attached after caping out (pull the skin up and out of the way), since the head will help hold the animal in position for field dressing and skinning.

Taking the cape. The caribou has a large, easily stained white mane to deal with. To keep it clean, remove the cape before field dressing. With the animal lying on its side, use a sharp knife to cut through the skin all around the animal's body just back of the forelegs. Circle cut around the forelegs about 8 inches from the point of attachment. Cut up the back of the leg to the initial caping cut to include the upper leg skin in the cape.

Then slit the back of the neck to a point about 4 inches from the ears. Make a Y cut from this cut to the base of the antlers. Now go back to the initial caping cut and work the skin from the shoulders, pulling it forward over the neck to the head. It will go more easily if you can turn the animal onto its back. Peel the skin forward to the base of the head. At this point you could sever the

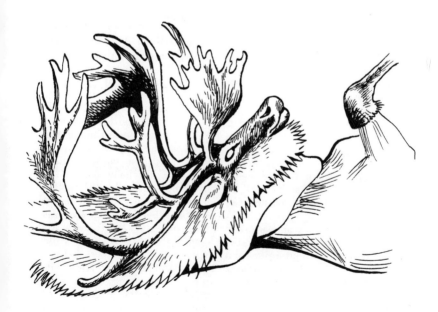

Be sure to pull the cape forward so that it doesn't get bloody. Keep the body on a piece of plastic or on logs found at the site.

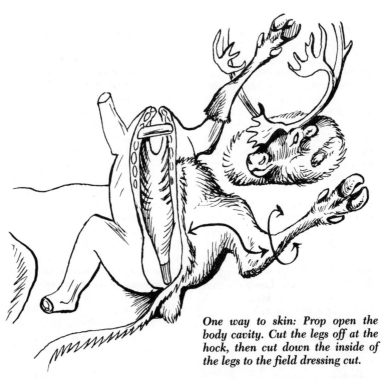

One way to skin: Prop open the body cavity. Cut the legs off at the hock, then cut down the inside of the legs to the field dressing cut.

neck, but with caribou it's often better to leave the head attached until you've finished skinning the body.

If you have to skin out the head in the field, follow the directions in the section on caping antlered game. Saw the antlers from the skull after the head is skinned out, and scrape off the velvet. The antlers will be bone white, but the taxidermist can stain them.

Gutting. With the animal on its back, cut off the scrotum. Slice the penis loose without cutting it off and pull it back between the hindlegs. Continue to cut between the hindlegs to the pelvic bone. Use a saw or hatchet to cut through the pelvic bone, and spread the hindlegs to expose the rectal and urethral tubes.

You may have to cut the stomach muscles just forward of the pelvis.

Next, circle cut around the anus (and vagina if you have a female). Pull the tubes forward and tie them off. Open the belly by carefully slicing forward from the pelvis to the ribs. Hold the belly muscles away from the intestines with your forefingers. Continue this cut through the breastbone to open the entire abdominal and chest cavity. Prop open the chest cavity with a stick. Then reach in the chest and sever the windpipe. Pulling on the windpipe and cutting tissue where needed, pull the lungs and heart from the chest cavity. Then cut the diaphragm. Roll the stomach and intestines out. The liver and heart are edible; slice them open and wash them with cold water as soon as possible. If you can, roll the body over to let blood drain.

Alternative 1. Now quarter the animal or bone it out as you would an elk, or use this alternative method, which allows you a more comfortable working position. Place the animal on its back and secure it with blocks placed on either side. The head will help keep the carcass in position. Start by cutting off the four legs at the knee and hock joints. Cut down the inside of each leg to the field dressing cut and start peeling the skin away from the legs, cutting tissue where needed. Remove the skin from the animal's sides down to the back. Leave the skin under the meat to keep it clean. Now cut the carcass in half, leaving one rib on the back half.

After the animal is cut in half, cut off the head and the neck ahead of the shoulder. Lay the cape, head, and the neck out of the way for now. Now finish skinning the front half as you turn it up on end. Then either cut the legs off at the shoulder joint or divide the front end in half down the center.

Now cut the rear half into manageable portions. Move the hips from side to side, peeling the skin off. You'll have to cut off the tail at the base to free the skin completely. Sever the hindlegs at the shank joint and the hip joint. Divide the back into a rump and loin section to reduce the size still further, if needed.

Alternative 2. The caribou carcass is sometimes cut up for transporting by this procedure. Roll the animal on its back and prop it securely. Start skinning out the carcass by cutting off the four legs at the knee and hock joints. Cut down the inside of each leg to the field dressing cut and start peeling the skin away from the legs,

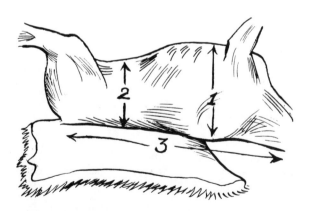

Alternative 2: After skinning down to the back, cut the animal into three pieces. Roll it over and finish skinning out the back. Then you can cut the carcass into more manageable portions.

one side at a time, pulling it down to
the back as far as possible.

Now cut the carcass into three
sections (you may need a saw). Make
the first cut immediately behind the
shoulders. Make the second cut just
behind the last rib. Then cut off the
neck at the head and at the shoulders. Roll the carcass to finish skinning out the back. Separating the
front legs and hindlegs from the carcass at the shoulder and hip joints
will make the remaining sections
small enough to carry from the field
in a packframe.

If the sections are still too heavy,
cut them through the center of the
backbone to divide the carcass into
six parts. If the backbone can't be
split, cut beside it through the ribs
and scapula.

Moose

Range. The moose is found in Alaska, all of the Canadian provinces, Maine, Vermont, New Hampshire, Michigan, Wisconsin, Minnesota, and the western states of Idaho, Montana, Wyoming, Colorado, Washington, and Utah.

Size. The moose is the second-largest hoofed animal in North America—only the bison is larger. The adult male is 8 to 9 feet long and about 70 to 75 inches tall at the withers. The female is smaller, about 6½ to 8 feet tall. Bulls weigh 850 to 1,200 pounds; adult females, 750 to 800 pounds.

Pelage. The general color of the winter coat is dark brown, sometimes almost black. The back, shoulders, neck, and head tend to be slightly paler than the flanks. The face is grayish; the lower belly and insides of the legs, light gray. In summer the pelage is somewhat lighter. The calf is reddish brown until it is about one year old, when it turns to its adult color; it does not have spots.

The moose has huge palmated antlers that it sheds every year. The "bell" that hangs from the throat occurs in both sexes but is more pronounced in the male.

Behavior. Moose are inclined to live within a certain area. They might spend months within a 1-square-mile area and a year or more within a 5- to 6-mile radius. They usually stay alone, but will congregate where food supplies are good. Moose are most active at daybreak and nightfall, but do move around at intervals during the night and may be up and about nearly anytime during the day.

With its long legs and large hooves, the moose can walk across swamps and muskegs that would be impassable to man and most other animals. It walks about 6 miles per hour and usually runs about 25 miles per hour, but can reach 35 miles per hour if badly frightened. It can swim 10 miles or more.

The moose's eyesight is poor, but its senses of hearing and smell are excellent.

Bulls grunt and bellow during the rutting, and cows moo. Calves bleat and cry in a high-pitched voice if they are uncomfortable.

Habitat. Moose are forest creatures, preferring to live where upland forest is interspersed with swamps, lakes, and streams or rivers. They do better in young, regenerating forests because they can find more food in immature trees than in mature forests. In summer they spend a great deal of time in water; in winter they frequent willow thickets and other heavy cover.

Food. Moose feed in ponds up to 12 feet deep; to eat, they stick their heads underwater or submerge completely. Broadleaf and bullrush pondweeds are preferred foods. Moose also graze on many upland grasses; sometimes they have to kneel to reach the grass because of their long front legs. They browse many different shrubs and trees, nipping off good-sized twigs and gnawing the bark. In some areas, the twigs and bark of aspen make up almost their entire food supply. Birch is also an important food in winter, but in some river bottom areas, moose subsist to a great extent on willow.

Reproduction. Female moose become sexually mature at two to four years of age. Bulls also become mature by this age but are usually prevented from breeding by the older, larger bulls. The rutting season occurs from late September to November. The gestation period is 240 to 246 days; usually a single calf is born, although twins or even triplets frequently occur. Calves stay with their mothers the first year.

Moose commonly live ten to twelve years.

Moose

A large bull moose is bigger than an elk and is a worrisome animal to field dress. But a small block and tackle can help you maneuver the animal, and a small saw or hand axe will deal with the thick bones. Carrying these tools is no problem because moose hunting is often done from boats or on horseback. A hunter on foot should pack a game saw and 50 feet of ¼-inch nylon rope.

Taking the cape. Usually a moose's large head and antlers are caped out and the head cut off before the animal is gutted. Cut through the skin all around the body just behind the hump between the shoulders, then cut around the front legs 6 inches from the point of attachment. Cut up the back of the neck to a point between the ears and then to the base of each antler. Work the skin off the shoulders down to the breast-

Cape the moose before you gut it. With the animal on its side, cut around the body just behind the shoulder hump. Cut around the front legs, and then make the standard slits on the back of the neck.

Roll the moose on its back to cut it more easily. Use a fallen tree as a pry pole.

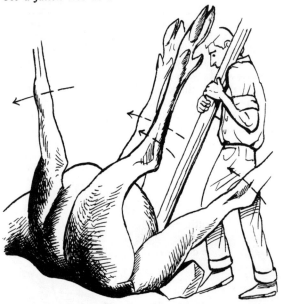

bone. Cut the head off at the base of the skull. If transportation is not available, you might have to skin out the head and leave it in the field: The huge antlers and cape will be heavy enough.

After you've cut off the head, start skinning at the back of the neck. Work toward the ears, following the instructions given for caping antlered game. Cut the ears from the skull. Then, using just the tip of the knife or a screwdriver, free the skin around the base of the antlers and work forward. When the skin is free from the antlers and forehead, skin out the eyes. Now skin out the muzzle to the nostrils, inserting your fingers in the muzzle so that you can

feel the path for the knife. Continue cutting forward until the upper lip is free. After the cape has been removed, turn the ears inside out and remove the cartilage. Then salt the cape.

Chop or saw the antlers from the skull by making a horizontal cut from the eye sockets to the back of the head.

Turning the carcass. Field dress this big animal as soon as you've finished caping so that the body heat will dissipate and not spoil the meat. It's easiest if you turn the moose over on its back.

To make the animal manageable, sever the front and rear legs at the knee and hock joints with a hunting knife. Then find an assortment of fallen logs and rocks to use as blocks. Lift up the front leg that's underneath and slide a block under it to hold it in place. Then raise the rear leg and do the same thing. Keep alternating back and forth. You can use a fallen tree as a pry pole. Push the end of the tree under the body, lift upward, then kick the blocks under the body. After it is halfway up, grasp the legs and roll it the rest of the way. Steady it with props and ropes.

Field dressing. Field dress using either the procedures outlined for elk or the following method, which works well if you can roll the moose onto its back, thus letting the intestines settle away from the belly skin and making the knife cuts less risky.

It also lets you work in a natural position.

First, cut the scrotum off at the base. Some hunters retain the testicles for food. Next, make a cut on each side of the penis. Pull it back between the hindlegs and lay it out of the way. Now circle cut around the anus (and vagina if the animal is female) to free the urethra and rectum from the hide.

Then slice deeply into the crotch to the pelvic bone. Cut into the abdominal wall very carefully. Cut the animal from the crotch to the breastbone, using your fingers to guide the knife.

Remove the rectum and urethra by cutting around the tissue that holds them in place. Split the pelvic bone. If a saw is not available, use a

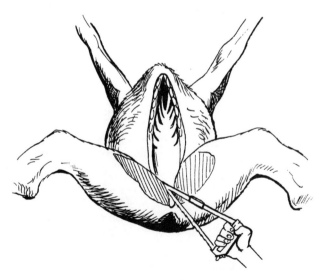

The pelvis is too massive to split with a knife. Use a saw or an axe.

wooden club to drive a hunting knife
or axe down the center of the pelvic
bone.

When you've freed the rectum
and bladder tubes and tied the ends
off, cut the diaphragm. Then pull
out the paunch and the rest of the
abdominal contents.

Open the chest as far as possible
by cutting up the center of the
breastbone. Then reach forward and
cut the windpipe and esophagus off.
Pull the heart and lungs out of the
body. Soak up blood with dry grass
or anything else at hand.

Quartering. If you don't care to
keep the moose skin intact, quarter
the animal with the skin on to keep
the meat clean until you get home.
Cut between the last two ribs from
the belly to the backbone and saw
or chop through the backbone to
divide the animal in two pieces.
Now stand the halves on end and
split them down the center of the
backbone to quarter the animal.

If you have to backpack the animal out and the quarters are too big
to manage, you can skin and bone
them out as (see *Elk*). If the moose is
lying on its side, follow the methods
outlined for skinning elk in the field.
You can also skin the quarters and
divide them into standard butchering cuts with a saw if you prefer not
to bone them.

Trophies and Furbearers

Black bear

Range. The black bear is found in every contiguous state (with the possible exceptions of Delaware and New Jersey), every province in Canada, and Alaska.

Size. The boar black bear is 54 to 70 inches long and weighs 250 to 500 pounds, but a few grow to 600 pounds or more. The sow is 50 to 58 inches long and weighs 225 to 450 pounds.

Pelage. The black bear is entirely covered with coarse hair except for the nose, eyes, and armpits (under the forelegs). The hair is usually black, but brown, red-brown, and white colorings also occur. In the northwestern United States, brown and red-brown (cinnamon) bears are common. A well-fed black bear has a shiny coat.

Behavior. Bears are wary, solitary animals that avoid man and shun other bears, except during the breeding season or when an unusual abundance of food in a particular location causes them to congregate.

The bear is active for about eight months a year, but with the onset of cold weather, it digs a den or makes a nest under an uprooted tree or fallen log, and crawls in for the winter. This inactive period is often called hibernation, although the bear does not truly hibernate. Instead, it just sleeps off and on.

A black bear can walk about 5 miles per hour and gallop about 32 miles per hour for an hour or more. It is most active from about an hour before dark until an hour after daylight, but might feed during midday also.

Bears growl, snort, and hiss when aroused.

Habitat. Black bears are usually found in heavily wooded terrain and brushland combined with some wetland; in the southeastern United States, they live in extensive wooded swamps.

Food. Black bears are omnivorous. In spring they eat emerging grass, young aspen leaves, and buds. Bears sometimes catch go-phers, squirrels, the young of other animals and birds, and birds' eggs, but they get most of their protein from ants and grubs found in rotting logs and stumps.

They are fond of fruit and berries, and each bear knows where to find the blueberries, raspberries, and blackberries in its territory. Bears also climb trees to get apples and cherries. In late summer and fall they feed heavily on acorns, beechnuts, and other large seeds or nuts. They are also fond of such farm crops as corn and wheat, and they occasionally kill pigs and calves or sheep.

Reproduction. Sows can breed when they are three and a half years old, although some breed when two and a half years old. Boars are capable of breeding when three years old, and probably do, since the sow is highly promiscuous and usually mates with several boars.

Mating occurs in June or July, and the gestation period is 225 days. The young are born in January or early February, while the mother is in her winter den. She usually births twins, but triplets also are common. About one litter in seven results in only one cub, and about one in ten litters produces four or more cubs. A litter of six was once observed in Wisconsin.

Cubs are only about 8 inches long and weigh 7 to 12 ounces when born. They develop slowly at first and their eyes don't open for about twenty-five days. At two months the cubs weigh 5 to 6 pounds; at twelve months, 40 to 75 pounds. The cubs stay with their mother for a year or even longer, denning with her or digging a den near the mother's lair.

Black bears commonly live twenty years but have a potential longevity of thirty years.

Black bear

After your bear is dead, drag it to a place where the grass is short and there is enough room for you to work. Make sure your knife is sharp and that you have plastic bags for the edible organs.

Before you field dress the bear, take photographs of it from at least four angles for the taxidermist. Also take the following measurements: length from nose to tail; length from nose to base of skull; circumferences of neck, forearm, chest, and belly; and length of tail.

Gutting. Place the bear on its back, blocking it in place if necessary.

Straddle or stand beside the animal's chest, feel for the solar plexus, and cut through the skin and muscle to open the chest cavity. The viscera do not touch the chest wall if the animal is lying on its back, but be careful not to cut too deeply. Next, slice through the breastbone, and spread the ribs to expose the chest contents. You may have to sever the diaphragm.

Remove the heart and lungs through this opening. Reach into the chest and feel for the windpipe and esophagus, cut through the windpipe, and pull on it to remove the lungs and heart. The heart is edible.

Now place two fingers in the chest opening to guide the knife and lift the belly skin, and slice the bear open from the chest to the crotch down the centerline of the belly. If the bear is a boar, slice on each side of the penis, but don't cut it off. When it is free, tie it off with string to keep urine from leaking on the carcass. Continue the cut to the anus, or to the external female organs if the bear is a sow.

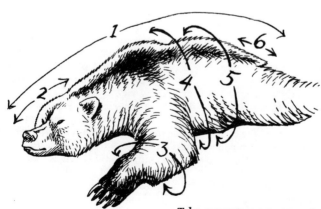

Take accurate measurements if you want a bear rug or a body mount.

59

A bear can be opened fairly easily at the sternum.

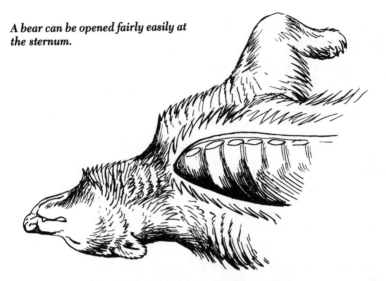

Split the pelvic bone with a sturdy knife or a small meat saw and remove the colon and urethra. Spread the hindlegs and cut the rectal and bladder tubes free by making a circle cut around the anus and female organs.

Lift the intestines out. Find the liver and kidneys, cut them loose, and put them in a plastic bag. Some bear hunters swear that kidneys are the best part of the bear. Be sure to remove and save the gall bladder (a bag containing a green liquid), attached to the liver. Bear gall is a valuable trade item.

Then turn the animal over and let the blood drain from the body cavity for at least 10 minutes. If clean water is available, wash out the body cavity, or wipe it out with paper towels. If you wish, leave a thin film of blood; it seals the meat.

Another way. If your knife isn't sturdy enough to open the breastbone or split the pelvis, you can dress the bear this way. Open the chest and abdomen by slitting the bear from crotch to rib cage. If the bear is a male, cut around the penis to free it from the belly. Without cutting it off, lay it back out of the way, still connected by its attachment through the pelvic bone. Now, using the point of the knife, circle cut around the anus (and vagina if the bear is female) deep enough so that the cut extends completely through the pelvic opening and can be seen inside the body cavity. If you make the cut correctly, you can pull the rectal and bladder tubes back through the opening to the inside of the cavity.

Pull the intestines out of the body cavity, cutting whatever tissue holds them in place, and then remove the contents of the chest cavity. Back at camp, split the pelvis as soon as possible so that the hindlegs can be spread for cooling the meat.

Skinning. How you skin the bear depends on the use you have in mind. If you're taking it to a taxidermist, leave the head and paws. For a tanner, skin out the head and paws. If you'll do the tanning yourself, skin out the paws and head, then salt and roll or freeze the hide.

Move the bear to a location suitable for skinning and butchering. If you have help, you can drag a bear like a deer, pulling a rope tied around its neck, or you can use a wheelbarrow. Be sure to place a large piece of plastic under the bear to keep the meat from getting dirty.

The most common way is to leave the head and paws on the skin. Lay the animal on its back and extend the field dressing cut forward to the junction of the head and neck. Then go to the rear of the animal and, 6 inches forward from the vent, slit the inside of each hindleg to the ankle joint between the paw and leg. Also slit the inside of each front leg from the field dressing cut to the wrist joint.

Now, starting at the junction of the field dressing cut and one hindleg, lift a flap of skin and slice the tissue underneath to free the hide from the meat.

Continue until you've freed the skin from the upper legs and the belly. You can usually lay the hide out flat. Skin out each of the lower legs to the paw. At the last joint, sever the paw from the leg, but don't cut the skin. The paw should dangle from the skin. Then skin out the neck as much as possible and cut off the head at the last joint of the neck. Leave the head in the skin.

You'll have to roll the bear from side to side to finish the skinning.

Skinning out the head. Whether you are going to tan the hide yourself

Start skinning the bear at the field dressing cut. Leave the head and paws in the hide if you're taking it to a taxidermist.

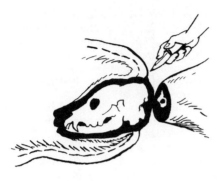

Cut the skull from the carcass at the last neck joint.

or send the bearskin to a tannery, you must also skin out the paws and head. Extend the leg cuts through the center of the paws. Then cut off the pad and carefully remove the flesh and foot bones. The claws are left on the skin; sever them at the last joint of the foot.

To skin out the head, extend the belly cut forward through the lower lip. Then lay back the skin from the cut. The skin lies tighter to the head than to any other part of the body, and every inch must be carefully shaved away from the tissue holding it to the head. Cut the ears off at the base and turn them inside out, cutting away the cartilage. Leave the lips on the hide, but skin them out. Also skin out the nose, keeping the black outer skin and removing as much cartilage as you can.

Fleshing and salting. After you've completely removed the hide, flesh it to remove as much fat as you can, and freeze, salt, or take it to the taxidermist as soon as possible. Untreated bear hide spoils very rapidly.

Use 1 pound of noniodized salt to 1 pound of hide. A bear hide weighs from 10 to 20 pounds. Lay the hide out flat, hair side down. Pour salt into the center of the hide, distribute it evenly all over the hide to the edges, and rub it in well.

Then fold the skin in half and roll it up. The salt will draw moisture from the hide, so incline one end to let the moisture run out. After about four days, unroll the hide, scrape off the old salt, and resalt it, using about the same amount of salt. Roll the hide up again and leave it for two more days. After that it will keep indefinitely if unrolled and tacked, hair side down, to a sheet of plywood to dry. Sprinkle borax on both sides to deter insects and predators.

Butchering. The carcass can be butchered into chops, roasts, and stew meat. Most cooks do not use bear meat for steaks because it needs slow cooking and moist heat. Quarter the animal and cut it up as you would a deer.

Timber wolf

Range. Wolves are listed as an endangered species but are thriving in some areas. Most wolves are found in Alaska, the southern Canadian provinces, and Minnesota. Many Western states have some wolves, at least on a temporary basis. Wisconsin has a small but stable pack.

Size. The length of the adult wolf, including the tail, is 58 to 65 inches. The adult males weigh 65 to 100 pounds and average about 75 to 85 pounds. Exceptionally large males may weigh over 100 pounds. Females are about 10 percent smaller.

Pelage. Generally, a wolf's upperparts are gray overlaid with black from the rump to the nape, and the head is often mixed gray and yellowish brown or cinnamon. The underparts are off-white to buff with a scattering of dark hairs, and the ears are cinnamon to tawny. On the chin and upper throat, the color varies from white to blackish. Outer parts of the legs are cinnamon buff to cinnamon; the forelegs often have a black line. The tail is grayish above, suffused with black and buff on the underside. But timber wolves vary in color from almost all white to almost all black. Wolf pups are sooty gray with brown heads.

Behavior. Wolves are frequently found in packs, often composed of related animals that stay together for hunting.

The wolf has excellent senses of eyesight, hearing, and smell, and is almost completely nocturnal, unless hunger drives it to hunt during the day. It is very strong for its size and possesses almost unbelievable endurance. A lone wolf is known to have killed a moose ten times its size.

Wolves are excellent communicators; they howl, bark, growl, and whine to send messages to other wolves.

The wolf can run about 28 miles per hour for a short distance but often pursues prey at about 18 to 20 miles per hour. It can swim well and occasionally enters water to catch food.

Habitat. Timber wolves generally live in large wilderness areas. In a few northern states, packs are established in large cutover areas that have grown back to thick forest.

Food. Timber wolves kill most of their food, although they may eat carrion if live food is scarce. The preferred food is deer, followed by moose, caribou, elk, and even bison. Where available, the beaver is a well-utilized summer food; snowshoe hares are taken in winter if big game is scarce. In some areas, wolves eat rodents almost exclusively, and all wolves eat berries, birds' eggs, grass, tree leaves, pine needles, and shrubs.

Reproduction. The timber wolf has a complicated mating ritual, which starts when one male establishes his dominance over the others in his pack by fighting. The dominant male then selects a mate. As a general rule, only this pair will breed. The rest of the pack helps to care for the young and teach them to hunt.

Wolves can breed when they are three years old. Breeding takes place in February or March, and the gestation period is sixty-three days long. The whelps are born in April or May. Wolves usually birth four to ten young in a den on the ground or under a log or rock.

Wolves often mate for life and are very good parents. The father brings food to the mother when she is nursing and to the pups before they can fend for themselves. The young stay with their mother and father for the first year or longer.

Timber wolves can live twenty years, but most do not survive beyond twelve years of age.

Timber wolf

Timber wolves make rare and striking trophies. The taxidermist will probably want to skin the animal himself, so freeze the entire animal without skinning or eviscerating it, or keep it as cool as you can. If, however, the wolf is likely to spoil before you get it to the taxidermist, prepare the hide by the open-skinning method.

Timber wolves are used by the fur trade, too. When an animal is sold to the trade, it is case skinned like a coyote or fox. Being larger, however, a timber wolf is harder to handle.

Case skinning. Lay the animal on its back. Slit the hindlegs from the pad on each foot to the anus. Peel the skin from the legs, using pliers if necessary. Use the tip of the knife to cut tissue between the skin and leg muscle if needed. Start skinning the leg at the hock. When enough skin is loosened to get your hand between the leg bone and the skin, pull it towards the foot pad. Carefully skin out the pad, leaving the last joint of the toe and the claw on the skin.

Slit the skin of the inside front legs from the foot pad to the knee. Then skin out the front feet, leaving the toe and claw on the skin. Pull the skin loose from the leg up to the knee. This will make it easier to free the front legs when the body skin is pulled to that point.

Now hang the wolf by its hindlegs at a comfortable working height, using stout ropes or heavy wire, or a commercial skinning gambrel. Work the skin loose around the base of the tail, slit the tail from the base to the end, and peel the skin from the

Hang the wolf securely and pull the hide down over the body.

tailbone. Cut off the testicles and sever the skin around the penis on a male wolf. Free the vagina and anus on the female by cutting the skin around them.

Now pull the skin down over the body to the shoulders. Then turn the leg skin inside out to remove the leg from the skin. The feet and lower legs are already skinned out so the skin should come off the shoulders easily.

Continue pulling the skin down over the animal's neck to the head. The neck is difficult, and the head will be even harder to skin out. Cut off the ears at the base, and cut carefully around the eyes and mouth. Cut the nose cartilage off at the end of the muzzle.

So as not to make holes in the head skin, cut against the bone, leaving the strips of flesh on the skin. You can flesh out the skin after you remove it, when it is easier to tell the skin from the excess flesh. Now flesh the rest of the skin.

Pull the skin onto a wolf stretcher to dry, fur side in. Turn the skin after it has started to dry, so that the fur buyer can inspect it. Insert a wooden wedge and let the skin dry completely.

Open skinning. Case-skinned animals are difficult to mount, so taxidermists suggest the wolf be open skinned in the following way: Lay the animal on its back and slit the belly from the anus to the neck. Then cut the inside of each hindleg from the foot pad to the belly slit. Slit the front legs from the pad to the belly cut. Do not cut into the foot pad on either the front or the rear legs.

Work the skin loose from the legs and cut the feet off at the joint above the pad, without cutting through the skin. Pull the skin down over the sides and back. When you have finished loosening the skin around the base of the tail, sever the tailbone without cutting through the skin, leaving the bone in the tail. Sever the head at the base, leaving the neck skin intact. When you have finished, the feet, tail, and head will dangle from the skin. The taxidermist will skin out the appendages.

Since this skin will not be dried, it should be salted; if you use about 10 pounds of salt, the skin will be well coated. Even so, keep it cool or frozen until it is delivered to the taxidermist.

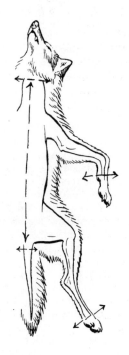

If you open skin, make these cuts.

Wolverine

Range. The wolverine's primary range is northern Canada and Alaska but it extends south to British Columbia and some western states. Wolverines have been seen as far south as northern California.

Size. The male wolverine is about 37 to 42 inches long, including the tail, and weighs 15 to 40 pounds. The female is 28 to 37 inches long and weighs 12 to 28 pounds.

Pelage. The wolverine's general color varies from dark brown to near black, but the cheeks, face, and forehead are tan. Two yellowish stripes begin at the shoulders, extend along the sides, and meet across the rump. This pattern produces a black circle on the back called a saddle.

Behavior. The wolverine is active year-round and has an extensive range for such a small animal—often 30 miles or more in diameter. Top speed is only 10 miles per hour, but the animal can travel at a slower rate for many miles without tiring. Its gait is a series of jumps like a weasel's. It usually stays on the ground but can climb trees.

Although primarily nocturnal, the wolverine is often active in daylight. It has an excellent sense of smell, average hearing ability, and poor eyesight. It is a fierce fighter when cornered but will avoid a fight when it can. Females with young may attack if molested. It is silent except for grunts and growls when feeding or disturbed.

The wolverine is solitary, except for mating pairs and a mother with kits. It is on the move almost constantly, seeking food, but usually has a home den that it returns to from time to time.

Habitat. Tundra and treeless areas are the wolverine's primary habitat, but it also occupies large forested areas in parts of its range.

Food. The wolverine is primarily a meat eater and will consume nearly any game animal or bird it can catch. In most areas, small animals, such as snowshoe hares, beavers, woodchucks, squirrels, chipmunks, and mice, are customary prey. But the wolverine will also kill big game that is weakened, crippled, or handicapped by deep snow. It eats berries in season, and it consumes small quantities of grasses or forbs.

Reproduction. Wolverine sows breed in their second year; the breeding season is in midsummer. Like others of the weasel family, the wolverine has delayed implanting of the embryo, which doesn't start to grow until late January. The young are born in early April. Usually two young are birthed, but sometimes triplets occur. Four young have been recorded. The young stay with the mother until fall.

Wolverines live eight to ten years in the wild but have a potential longevity of eighteen years.

Wolverine

Wolverines make appealing full-sized mounts, and local taxidermists, sports shops, and state game department people want wolverines to mount. Trappers' organizations also get such requests. You may be able to sell the carcass unskinned; if not, proceed to skin and stretch the hide for tanning or for the fur trade.

Wolverines are skinned much like raccoons, except that the claws are left on the skin.

It is better to skin a wolverine outside or in a skinning shed because its rank-smelling musk gland could be accidentally cut, and its greasy skin could ruin furnishings.

Case skinning. Hang the wolverine up by the hindlegs at about eye level. Use wire or rope or a trapper's gambrel. With a sharp skinning knife, make a slit from the pad on the free hindleg down the inside of the hindleg to the vent. Circle cut around the anus. Avoid cutting the musk gland by making the cut wide. Skin out the paw, cutting the toes off at the last joint to leave the claw on the skin. Work the leg skin loose to the crotch. Then rehang the animal from the skinned-out leg and skin out the other paw and hindleg to the crotch. Now hang it by both legs. Work the skin loose at the base of the tail, slit the tail skin on the underside, and work the tailbone out of the tail skin.

When you've skinned out the hindlegs and tail, pull the skin inside out down over the body. You can often peel the skin down over the body without using the knife, but you may want to trim the fat and flesh from the skin as you proceed.

When the skin has slipped to the front legs, turn the skin of the legs inside out to pull the hide down to the foot pad. Then skin out the foot, leaving the claws on the skin.

Be careful of the wolverine's scent glands when you make the first cut across the back of the legs.

Continue to pull the skin to the head. Often the neck skin is tight; you may have to use the knife to cut tissue from the neck muscles so that the skin will come free. Stop at the ears. Cut them off at the base and continue to peel the skin over the skull to the eyes. Use the tip of the knife to cut the skin from the skull at the eyes. Cut the lips from the skull, and also cut off the nose cartilage to free the skin.

Fleshing. After the skin is off the animal, scrape it to remove all the flesh and fat. You can do this on a flat surface, laying the skin flesh side up and scraping it with a dull butcher knife, but a fleshing beam is easier to use.

The wolverine skin must now dry. Pull it over an extra-large raccoon or coyote stretcher, fur side in. Center the eyes and tail on one side of the stretcher, and the legs and mouth on the opposite side. Hold it in place by nailing the hindlegs and the base of the tail. Spread the tail out flat and tack it open to dry. After the skin has been on the stretcher a day or so, it will appear glazed. Take it off, turn it fur side out, and put it back on the stretcher. Place a wooden wedge between the belly skin and the drying board so that you can remove the hide easily. Leave the hide this time until it is completely dry.

Open skinning. If you want your trophy mounted but the wolverine carcass is likely to spoil before being delivered to the taxidermist, choose the open-skinning procedure (see *Mountain lion*). The open-skinned hide is much easier (and cheaper) to mount.

Skin out the paws, leaving the claws on the skin. Cut the paws from the skin at the last joint.

Mountain lion

Range. Most mountain lions, or panthers, are found from the eastern slopes of the Rocky Mountains west to the Pacific Ocean, north to British Columbia, and south to Mexico. But a small population still exists along the Gulf Coast from Texas to Mississippi, and there are a few in southern Florida. In recent years, mountain lions have also been sighted in Michigan, Wisconsin, Minnesota, and some eastern states.

Size. Individuals vary considerably in size. The adult male mountain lion may be 70 to 102 inches in length and about 26 to 30 inches high at the shoulder. It may weigh 65 to 235 pounds, but the average is about 160 pounds. The adult female is about 35 percent smaller, with an average weight of about 135 pounds.

Pelage. Mountain lions can range in color from cinnamon to slate gray, but the most common color phase is reddish brown on the upperparts and paler on the feet, upper lips, chin, and throat. The underparts can be almost white. The dorsal strip from the back of the head to the tip of the tail is darker than the general coloration and may be mixed with a few black hairs. The underside of the tail is lighter and may be almost white.

Mountain lion kittens are dull buff to almost orange with raccoonlike dark bands on their tails and blotches or spots on their bodies and heads. The dark bands and spots are gone by about six months of age.

Behavior. Mountain lions are secretive animals, living in remote areas by necessity and preference. They have excellent eyesight, above-average hearing, a fairly well developed sense of smell, and exceptionally sensitive whiskers. Mountain lions run about 20 miles per hour but can rush at greater speeds when they are catching prey. They can swim for a mile or more and jump 15 feet vertically.

Lions are primarily nocturnal but hunt or move in daylight as well. They are exceptionally wary of man and of dogs, which they probably associate with man. Like most predators, they are solitary except during the mating season.

Mountain lions scream, purr, and growl.

Habitat. Mountain lions almost always live in large tracts of unsettled territory with a steady supply of big game. But they can adapt to widely differing climates and terrains, from arid regions to swamps and from large forests to open, almost treeless mountain ranges.

Each lion claims a large territory. The male may have a travel route 50 to 100 miles in diameter; the female's range is about half as large. It often has a home den or cave.

Food. When abundant, deer are the mountain lion's primary food, but it also eats small animals—porcupines, rabbits, hares, and gophers—and even fish. It also preys on domestic stock and usually is not tolerated in agricultural areas. Occasionally a mountain lion kills a moose or elk. It covers its kill with grass and twigs and returns to eat until the carcass is devoured, unless it has made another kill in the meantime.

Reproduction. Mountain lions breed when they are three years old. They do not have a definite breeding period, but most females appear to come in heat between December and March. They breed every other year, often with the same mate. Fights between males over females have been observed.

The gestation period is ninety-one to ninety-seven days. Usually two kittens are born, although litters of one to six have been recorded. A newborn weighs about 1 pound and is about 10 inches long. At six months the young weigh about 30 pounds each and are able to care for themselves; nevertheless, they may stay with the mother for a year or even more.

Mountain lions can live to fourteen years or more, although most do not survive more than seven years in the wild.

Mountain lion

After the mountain lion is down, take photos of it from several angles. Get closeups of the lion's head from a low viewpoint and from an upper angle, as well as straight on. Shoot some closeups of the lion's foot, especially from the top down.

Then measure the cat's length from the head to the tail, and from the mouth to the back of the skull. Also measure its height at the shoulder, the width and circumference of its neck, and the size of its feet and pads.

Gutting. To retard spoiling, some hunters eviscerate the lion before skinning, but it's not necessary since the lion is rarely eaten. If you fear the carcass might spoil and ruin the skin, follow these procedures.

First, cut off the genitals, or if a female, circle cut around the vagina and anus. Then slit the animal up

the center of the belly to the chest. Stop the cut between the front legs, since the skin shouldn't be opened any farther at this point. Scoop the intestines out, and reach forward to the front of the chest cavity and cut off the esophagus. Pull the guts out and discard them. Prop the body cavity open so that it will cool. Pack it with ice, if it's available, and transport the cat as soon as possible to a cooling facility.

Rough skinning. Most lions are rough skinned in the field. The hide is removed but the paws and head are left on the skin.

Start skinning as soon as possible after the kill. When the animal is still warm, the skin will peel easily from the body. Wipe the blood from the animal, turn it on its back, and slit it up the center from the anus to the lower jaw. Make sure this cut

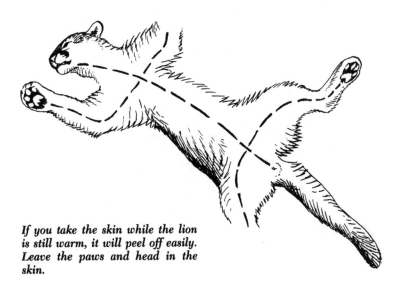

If you take the skin while the lion is still warm, it will peel off easily. Leave the paws and head in the skin.

goes only through the skin. Slit the skin up the inside of each front and rear leg from the center cut to the pad.

Start peeling the skin back at the junction of the belly cut and a leg cut. Use the knife to cut tissue only when the skin can't be pulled from the body. Skin out the legs and cut the foot off at the last joint, leaving the foot in the skin.

Peel the skin off the hips to the base of the tail and then cut the tailbone, leaving it in the skin (the tail will still be connected to the body skin). Pull the skin to the head and cut the head off at the last neck joint, leaving the skull in the skin. When you're finished, the feet, tail and skull will still be in the skin.

Flesh the hide and salt it, using about 15 pounds of salt. Spread the skin out, hair side down, pour the salt in the center of the skin, and spread it around, rubbing it well into all parts of the skin. It will keep about one week after salting, even in warm weather.

Finish skinning. You must completely skin out the hide if you plan to keep it for a long time without freezing, or if you're sending it to a tannery. This is painstaking and time-consuming work. Using a knife with a short blade, skin out the feet, separating the flesh and bones from the skin. Cut each toe off at the last joint, leaving the toenail on the skin.

Skin out the tail by slitting the underside from the base to the tip of the tail. Work the skin off the tail, using the tip of the knife to cut the connective tissue between the skin and the tailbone.

Remove the skull from the head skin by turning the skin inside out, slitting it up the neck only as much as necessary to continue. Cut the ears off at the base, right next to the skull. Use a screwdriver to help remove head skin. Push the blade between the skin and skull to loosen the skin without cutting it. Be careful to cut the tissue right against the skin so that the eyelids and eyebrows are left on the skin. Trim the nose cartilage against the bone, but leave the lips on the skin. Once the skin is free, remove the ear cartilage and extra flesh on the lips and nose by shaving a little at a time. Spread the skin out, hair side down, and rub salt into the flesh side. Roll up the skin and let it drain.

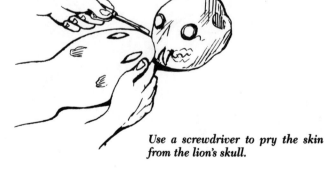

Use a screwdriver to pry the skin from the lion's skull.

One of a Kind

Javelina

Range. The javelina is found in remote regions of south Texas, New Mexico, and Arizona, and in Mexico and other countries of Central America.

Size. The adult javelina is 28 to 36 inches long and 17 to 20 inches high at the shoulder. Adults weigh 30 to 45 pounds; exceptional individuals may reach 60 pounds.

Pelage. Javelinas are grizzled gray-black with a lighter collar. Texas animals are very dark and have a faint collar; Arizona and New Mexico javelinas are lighter in color with a distinct, near-white collar. The collar circles the neck in front of the shoulders and extends to the rear along the back. Baby javelinas are yellowish black to reddish with a black stripe down the back.

Behavior. The javelina can walk at a fairly rapid rate and run 20 to 25 miles per hour for a short distance, but it usually moves slowly across prickly pear flats and thornbush thickets, rooting in the soil for food and staying in cover. The javelina's sense of smell is sharp, but its hearing is only fair and its eyesight is poor.

Javelinas usually travel in bands of three to a dozen or more animals. They are diurnal animals but may feed at night during extremely hot weather.

Javelinas snort, snuffle, and squeal.

Habitat. Javelinas often live in arid regions, wandering among brushy draws and rimrock crevices where cactus, mesquite, and desert shrubs grow. But they also thrive in grassland and live-oak regions in Texas, and even at the edges of swamps or wetlands. They must have a source of water in their territory, although they get some moisture from their food.

Food. Javelinas will eat almost anything organic but get most of their food by grubbing for roots and tubers. They also graze prickly pear cactus, acorns, and grass when they can find it in their habitat.

Reproduction. A sow javelina breeds when she is about a year and a half old but often loses her first litter. A month or so after losing a litter, she breeds again. She has no fixed breeding season and may come in heat anytime. The gestation period is twenty to twenty-one weeks long, and usually one or two 1-pound piglets are born. Two hours after they are born, the piglets can outrun a man. The sow leaves the band to give birth but rejoins it in a day or two.

Javelinas often live four or five years, although they have the potential to live ten years or more.

Javelina

Most javelinas are killed when the weather is warm, so they should be caped and field dressed without delay to prevent spoilage. Although some hunters remove the musk gland first, it is really not necessary, as the gland will come off with the skin. The musk gland is located about 6 inches forward of the base of the tail on the animal's back. Avoid touching the gland with the skinning knife or your hands, which could transfer off-flavors to the meat. If you want to remove the gland first, follow these steps: Cut deep into the flesh and muscle surrounding the gland, lift it out, and discard it. Clean the knife before proceeding, in case it nicked the gland.

Hang the javelina from a tree — it's the easiest way to work. Slit the skin of one or both hindlegs at the heel, pass stout rope under the thick gambrel cords, wrap it around the leg to make a secure attachment, and suspend the animal. If you must work on the ground, remember to lay plastic under the animal.

Caping out. Skin the cape before going any further. Many javelinas have white manes that are easily stained.

Remove the cape first by cutting completely around the body about 5 inches behind the front legs. Cut off the front legs at the knee joint and peel the cape skin forward over the head. Take it off by pulling on the skin and using the tip of the knife to cut tissue as necessary. When you reach the ears, cut them off at the base under the skin. Cut

The javelina is small and can be hung up to remove the cape. Cape it much as you would antlered game, cutting around the body and legs first, then peeling the cape skin over the head. Cut out the scent gland at this time.

the eyelids, lips, and nose loose from the skull by severing the tissue between the skull and the skin.

Cut the head off at the base of the skull and trim the meat away from the skull bone, but take it with you because most taxidermists want the skull of the javelina as part of the mount. Trim the excess meat from the cape and salt both the cape and the skull. Keep the cape in a cool place until you can get to a taxidermist.

Gutting. Lower the javelina to the ground and gut it before skinning it further. First, make a cut just through the belly skin from the anus to the point where the head was removed. Then free the penis from its attachment, cut down between the rear legs to the pelvic bone, and split the pelvis with a knife or small hatchet. Circle cut around the anus and female sex organs to free the bladder and rectal tubes, pull them forward, and tie them off. Carefully cut the belly muscles just forward of the pelvic area to expose the intestines. Then use two fingers to guide the knife as you slit the belly open from the pelvis through the breastbone to the neck. Split the breastbone with a sturdy sharp knife.

Quickly take out the intestines and chest cavity contents. Then allow the animal to drain for several minutes before skinning.

Skinning. Hang the animal again and proceed with skinning. Work carefully; when tanned, the skin makes excellent leather. First, circle cut around the hindlegs below the rope attachment. Then slit down the inside of the hindlegs to the crotch.

Tying off the rectal tube will prevent leakage of the body fluids onto the meat.

Work the skin off the hindlegs by pulling downward from the circle cut, then pull it down over the body. The skin will strip easily in one piece if the animal is still warm. After you've removed the skin, scrape it to remove excess flesh and then salt it to keep it from spoiling.

The carcass can be cut into butchering cuts or taken whole to a professional butcher.

Like a hog. Some hunters handle the javelina like a domestic hog, scalding it to remove the hair and cutting up the meat with the skin attached. Do this as soon after the kill as possible.

Remove the intestines and scent gland from the javelina in the field.

Transport the animal home and keep it cool while you heat a large container of water to 150–170°F.

Lay the javelina on a bench on its side and cover it with burlap sacks. Pour hot water over the skin, soaking the burlap. After about 3 minutes, remove the burlap and scrape the hair from the skin with a dull knife blade. When the upper side of the javelina is scraped clean, turn it over and repeat the process.

Now the animal is ready for butchering.

After you've scalded the javelina, scrape off the hair with a dull knife or a paint scraper.

Alligator

Range. The American alligator is found only in the southeastern United States. It is common from North Carolina southward through Florida and westward to the Rio Grande River. Although the alligator was once an endangered species, more than a million were counted in the United States in the late 1980s.

Size. Alligators grow from about 9 inches long when hatched to as much as 18 feet. Most female alligators attain a length of 9 feet and weigh about 160 pounds. Male alligators commonly reach 11 to 12 feet and a weight of 450 to 550 pounds.

Pelage. The alligator resembles a huge lizard with short legs, a long tail, a streamlined body, and a broad rounded snout with a large tooth-filled mouth. Its large reptilian feet are equipped with long claws. The general coloration is grayish black, but young alligators have yellowish marks that sometimes persist into adulthood. The skin is covered with scalelike markings and has projections along the back, commonly called horns and buttons.

Behavior. The alligator is a mobile animal, able to run on land and to swim rapidly by moving its tail from side to side. It often digs a den in a bank from below the waterline to above water underground, which it uses for feeding and resting.

Both sexes spend most of their time resting and waiting for food to come by. They are usually solitary, but may congregate at a good food supply. In breeding season the sexes may be found together for extended periods.

Female alligators are generally silent, but males bellow loudly, often at night.

Habitat. The alligator is an aquatic animal, seldom venturing on land for any length of time. It lives in river systems and swamps, where it inhabits a favorite pond or pool. Coastal marshes are excellent habitat, but alligators seldom venture into salt water. Females live in vegetated, mostly secluded areas, but male alligators prefer open water. In winter both sexes burrow into the mud or go into deep-water dens to escape low temperatures.

Food. The young alligator eats mostly crawfish, crabs, and shrimp, but in certain seasons aquatic beetles and insect larvae make up an important part of the food supply. It also catches and eats fish, snakes, frogs, turtles, and mice.

Alligators more than 5 feet long will eat any animal inhabiting land or water that they can catch and kill. Muskrats, nutria, rabbits, and ducks and other waterfowl make up a large part of their diet. Unusually large alligators kill deer, pigs, dogs, cattle, and occasionally humans. They seize these large animals and drag them underwater to drown them, often leaving them until they are partially rotten and soft. They then tear the rotten prey apart with their teeth, grasping a body part of the prey and twisting their own bodies until that part comes off.

Reproduction. Female alligators are sexually mature when they're eleven years old, and they mate during the months of March, April, and May. When the male alligator finds a receptive female, he herds her into open water. During the breeding season males bellow loudly and fight other males.

After mating the female finds a secluded pond and makes a nest. She lays about fifty hard-shelled, white eggs that are slightly larger than hens' eggs. After the eggs are laid, she covers them and lets the heat of the sun incubate them. The female stays near the nest to protect the eggs from raccoons and other predators. The eggs hatch in about sixty days. The young alligators make grunting noises when they are hatching. When the female hears this, she uncovers the nest so that the young can find their way out. The young alligators immediately go into the water.

Alligators commonly live until they are fifty to sixty years old.

Alligator

Most hunters "fish" for alligators with a baited hook hung over the water. The higher the hook is hung, the larger the alligator expected to take the bait. After the alligator is caught, it is shot in the head or killed by a knife thrust to the vulnerable point just behind the head. It is then turned on its back and allowed to cool in a shady place for about an hour before skinning starts.

First steps. Place the alligator on its belly. Start the first cut at the top of the neck just behind the head, inside a natural line on the alligator's neck. Alligator skinners call it "following the dots," since this skin is dotted with spots. This first cut goes only as far as the lower jaw, and should not encircle the neck.

Next, separate the projections called horns, which run from the head to the tip of the tail, from the rest of the hide. They are left on the carcass. Starting at the neck cut, cut on either side of the horns along the back to the tip of the tail. Cut off and discard the last 3 inches of the tail.

Cut off the hindlegs at the ankle. Then make a cut up the back of the hindlegs from one ankle across the body behind the anus to the other ankle.

Finally, cut around the front feet at the wrists, pull the leg backward, and cut up the front of the leg. Extend this cut so that it joins the cut on either side of the horns.

Skinning. After you've made these initial cuts, you can begin the actual skinning, one side at a time. Start at one side of the neck and pull this section of the skin forward to re-

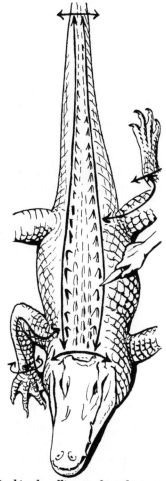

To skin the alligator, first slit across the head, then cut along the horns. Cut off the last 3 inches of the tail; sever the hindlegs at the ankle and the forelegs at the wrist. Slit the leg skin to the cuts on either side of the horns.

The lower jaw skin is retained. It should pull off after you've cut it.

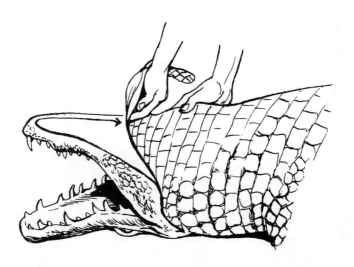

move the skin from the neck and shoulder. Alligator skin lies tight to the body and must be cut loose.

Then pull the skin from the front leg back to the hindleg. The legs will skin out easier if you hold them rigid with a bungee cord or rope while you skin. Use a pair of pliers to pull on the skin while you cut the tissue between the hide and meat.

When you've pulled the upper skin from the body, roll the alligator on its back. Cut along each side of the lower jaw from the neck to loosen the lower jaw skin. Also cut around the anal area. Then grasp the skin at the point of the jaw and pull it backward, peeling the skin off from front to back to take the belly skin off completely.

The hide must be carefully cured so that it does not develop "red meat," a type of spoilage that turns the inside red and causes the skin to separate into layers. Lay the hide flat and carefully scrape away all flesh and fat. Then go over the entire surface with a paint scraper, pushing hard against the hide to drive out as much fat as possible.

Next, salt the skin with non-iodized salt. A big alligator will take about 100 pounds. Lay the skin out, scale side down, and rub the salt hard enough to push it into the hide.

Then roll the hide up in the following way: Fold the leg skin inward, the tail skin forward from the tip for half its length, and the neck skin inward. This produces a strip. Starting from the forward end, roll the strip up as tightly as possible and tie it with stout cord. Then place the skin in a container and cover it with more salt. Allow the moisture drawn out of the skin to drain away.

Keep the skin in a cool place. After three days, unroll it, scrape off the crusted salt, and add a new layer. Roll up and tie as before. Alligator skins will also keep if frozen or placed in a very strong salt brine.

Gutting. Gut the alligator after you have removed the skin. Make a slit down the center of the belly from the lower jaw to the tail and remove all intestines and organs. The contents of an alligator's intestines have a rank, foul odor, so use great care not to puncture them. Leakage from a cut intestine would make the meat unfit to eat. Wipe the body cavity clean. Store the carcass in a cooler at a temperature lower than 45°F for at least 12 hours before butchering.

Butchering. The alligator has four main cuts of meat: jowls, legs, torso, and tail. First, remove the jowls by cutting them away from the cheekbone. They are a small but tasty cut of meat. Fillet the jowls from the cheekbone by scraping close to the bone with a sharp, flexible knife blade.

Remove the legs by cutting through the joint where the legs join the body. Cut the front legs at the shoulder, the rear legs at the pelvic joint. Then separate the muscles from the bone. Cut around the leg and scrape down along the bone. Leg meat is tough but tasty.

The torso meat extends from the lower neck to the end of the rib cage. The best part is the tenderloin, which lies along the backbone. Carve it away from the backbone in

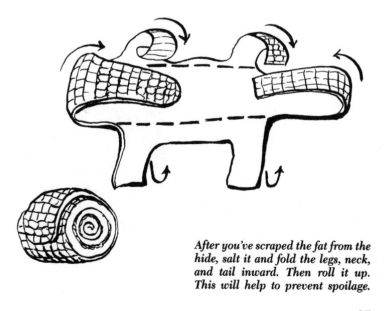

After you've scraped the fat from the hide, salt it and fold the legs, neck, and tail inward. Then roll it up. This will help to prevent spoilage.

87

two long strips. Carve the rib meat away from the bones.

Cut the tail off at the base, and butcher it by slicing it crossways into 1-inch-thick chops. Some say the very best part of the alligator is the cone-shaped tail muscles at the base of the tail.

Experienced alligator hunters often fillet the meat from the tail without even cutting the tail from the carcass. They take the meat off in four strips, since it lies in four sections around the X-shaped tail-bone.

Be sure to remove all fat and gristle from alligator meat; it is strong tasting and would render the meat inedible.

Trophies. Alligator heads are mounted like deer heads, and alligator feet are used for ashtrays. Alligator teeth are often used for making jewelry.

Choice cuts: When you're butchering the alligator, don't forget the tail meat and the meat on the jawbone.